First Ladies

Women Who Called the White House Home

★ BEATRICE GORMLEY ★

SCHOLASTIC INC.

New York Toronto London Auckland Sydney
Mexico City New Delhi Hong Kong Buenos Aires

To my mother, Elizabeth F. LeCount, the First Lady in my life

This book was originally published in hardcover by Orchard Books in 2001.

ISBN 0-590-25518-5
Text copyright © 1997 by Beatrice Gormley.
All rights reserved. Published by Scholastic Inc.

SCHOLASTIC and associated logos are trademarks and/or registered trademarks of Scholastic Inc.

12 11 10 9 8 7 6 5 4 3 2   4 5 6 7 8 9/0

Printed in the U.S.A.
First trade edition, March 2004

TABLE OF CONTENTS

INTRODUCTION

The term "First Lady" has been used to refer to the wife of the president of the United States since the Civil War Era. But what kind of people were the First Ladies? They were athletic and no-nonsense, like Bess Truman; they were sophisticated society beauties, like Jacqueline Kennedy; they were pioneer women, like Anna Harrison. They were artists, like Ellen Wilson; or businesswomen, like Lady Bird Johnson; or full-time invalids, like Ida McKinley. Their stories are funny, romantic, shocking, full of adventure — and sometimes tragic.

Some First Ladies, like Abigail Adams and Eleanor Roosevelt, were independent thinkers and personalities in their own right, whose husbands listened carefully to their opinions. Other First Ladies, like Mamie Eisenhower, stuck to a strictly limited role as wife and hostess. As for Helen Taft, she practically shoved her reluctant husband into the White House.

Julia Grant dreamed for years of becoming the president's wife, and wept when she had to leave the White House after two terms. Rachel Jackson, on the other hand, declared that she would "rather be a doorkeeper in the house of my Lord than to live in that palace at Washington."

One of the few things the First Ladies have in common is their devotion to their husbands. Presidents from John Adams to Bill Clinton have acknowledged how much they owe their accomplishments to their close, loving marriages.

Many presidents' wives have complained that being First Lady is like living in a glaring spotlight, with the whole world watching every move. As Rosalynn Carter warned Hillary Clinton, "You're going to be criticized no matter what you do, so be criticized for what you think is best and right for the country."

These are the stories of women who helped to shape the face of a nation.

A painting of
Martha Washington

Martha Dandridge Custis Washington

1731–1802

George Washington Administration,
1789–1797

Martha Dandridge was born on June 2, 1731, near Williamsburg, Virginia, the daughter of Frances Jones Dandridge and Colonel John Dandridge, a wealthy planter. Growing up, she learned to manage a large household and entertain guests, to play the spinet and ride horseback. Once she rode her horse into her uncle William's house and up the stairs, but her father refused to scold her. "She's not harmed William's staircase," he pointed out, "and by heavens, how she can ride!"

At the age of seventeen Martha married a planter, Colonel Daniel Parke Custis. They had four children: John Parke Custis and Martha Parke Custis, and two who died as babies.

Colonel Custis died when Martha Custis was twenty-five, leaving her to run the plantation. Many men would have liked to marry the attractive, rich widow, but when she met Colonel George Washington of the Virginia militia, she decided within days that they were perfectly suited. They were married in January 1759.

Colonel and Mrs. Washington settled down to the plantation life they both loved at Mount Vernon, their estate in Virginia. They had no children of their own, but he took guardianship of her son and daughter.

George and Martha Washington with their grandchildren

When the Revolution began in 1775, George Washington became commander in chief of the Continental Army. Every winter, as the war slowed down temporarily, Mrs. Washington joined her husband in camp. At Valley Forge during the winter of 1777–78, her heart went out to the sick, starving, ragged soldiers. She visited them every day, and she persuaded the other officers' wives to join her in patching the soldiers' clothes, knitting socks, and making shirts.

After the Revolution was won, General Washington was elected the first president of the United States of America. He and Mrs. Washington would rather have gone back to their pleasant life at Mount Vernon,

but they both felt he had a responsibility to the new nation.

Martha Washington disliked New York, the first capital of the United States, and she didn't like Philadelphia, the next capital, much better. In spite of this, she carried out her official entertaining duties in a gracious, low-key style. "Lady Washington" did not allow politics to be discussed at her receptions and dinners, and she ended evening events at nine o'clock so that President Washington could get his rest.

In 1797, at the end of her husband's presidency, Mrs. Washington happily returned to Mount Vernon. "The General and I feel like children just released from school," she wrote a friend. Only two years later, in 1799, George Washington became suddenly ill and died. Martha Washington had no heart to go on without him. She died of a fever on May 22, 1802, at the age of seventy-one, and was buried with President Washington at Mount Vernon.

A folk-art-style watercolor of George and Martha Washington, circa 1801

A portrait of Abigail Adams at age 22

ABIGAIL SMITH ADAMS
1744–1818

John Adams Administration, 1797–1801

Born on November 11, 1744, in Weymouth, Massachusetts, Abigail Smith was the daughter of Elizabeth Quincy Smith and William Smith, a Congregational parson. Abigail was bright and an avid reader, with a keen interest in politics, but since she was a girl, the current attitude of the day meant that she would never be allowed to attend college.

When she was seventeen Abigail met John Adams, a lawyer who was ten years older. He was away much of the time, following the circuit courts. Discovering their mutual interests in books and politics, they began exchanging long, lively letters. Abigail and John were married in 1764, at her father's parsonage in Weymouth, when she was nineteen.

In later years, when John joined the American resistance to the British, Abigail Adams heartily approved, although she had to take care of their four children — Abigail, John Quincy, Charles, and Thomas (another baby died in infancy) — and run their farm in Braintree (later called Quincy), Massachusetts, by herself. Mrs. Adams never minded hard work, but she missed her husband terribly.

From 1774 through 1777 John Adams served in the First and Second Continental Congresses in Philadelphia. In her letters, Mrs. Adams kept him up to date on politics in Massachusetts and told him her ideas, which were well ahead of their time, for shaping the new American government. In September 1774, she wrote about slavery: "It allways appeared a most iniquitous Scheme to me — fight ourselfs for what we are daily robbing and plundering from those who have as good a right to freedom as we have." In the spring of 1776, Mrs. Adams reminded her husband to "remember the ladies," meaning that women should be allowed the right to own property and be given protection against abusive husbands. Unfortunately, Mr. Adams did not take her advice on either slavery or women's rights.

During the Revolution, John Adams served as a diplomat in France for four long years. The Adamses wrote often, but it took months to deliver a letter from France to Massachusetts. In 1783, after the peace treaty between the United States and England was signed, Mrs. Adams took ship for a joyous reunion with her husband in London.

When John Adams was elected president in 1796, Abigail Adams was nervous about following "Lady Washington." But actually she held livelier social events, encouraging witty conversation and political discussion. She was the first president's wife to live in the White House, where she hung laundry in the unfinished East Room.

President Adams asked her opinion of his speeches before he gave them and, as always, he discussed the business of government with her. She was also the first president's wife to influence the press; Abigail Adams sent information favorable to the Adams administration to the newspaper editors.

When John Adams was defeated by Thomas Jefferson in the presidential election of 1800, both Adamses were

Abigail Smith Adams was the wife of one president and the mother of another.

indignant. However, Mrs. Adams was delighted to go back to running the farm in Braintree, where she could enjoy the company of her husband *and* her children and grandchildren.

Abigail Adams became sick with typhoid fever in October 1818. A few days later, she died at the age of nearly seventy-four, several years before her oldest son, John Quincy Adams, would become president. She is buried in Quincy, Massachusetts, and John Adams is buried beside her.

The Jeffersons' daughter, Martha

MARTHA WAYLES SKELTON JEFFERSON
1748–1782

Thomas Jefferson Administration, 1801–1809

Martha Wayles was born on October 30, 1748, in Charles City County, Virginia, daughter of Martha Eppes Wayles and John Wayles, a lawyer and landowner. Little is known about her life. At eighteen she married Bathurst Skelton, also a lawyer, who died when Martha was twenty-two. They had one son, who died as a young child.

At the time of her marriage to Thomas Jefferson on New Year's Day, 1772, when she was twenty-three, Martha Skelton was wealthy, with an estate of her own near Williamsburg. She was said to be beautiful, although no pictures of her have survived. She and Mr. Jefferson both loved music; he played the violin and she the harpsichord. According to Thomas Jefferson's autobiography, their life together at Monticello, their mountaintop estate, was "ten years in unchequered happiness."

But giving birth to six children (only two of whom, Martha and Mary, survived) seems to have strained Mrs. Jefferson's health. In addition, the years of the Revolution were extremely strenuous — twice she and her children were forced to flee from British invaders. After a long illness, she died on September 6, 1782.

Mr. Jefferson was crazed with grief, staying in his room for three weeks and pacing until he dropped down exhausted. "The violence of his emotion," his older daughter, Martha, wrote later, " . . . I dare not trust myself to describe."

Thomas Jefferson never remarried. During his years as minister to France, his two daughters kept him company in Paris. By the time he became president in 1801, his wife had been dead for nineteen years.

When he needed a hostess, President Jefferson often asked his secretary of state's wife, Dolley Madison, to preside at White House dinners. The president's daughter Martha Randolph also acted as

A portrait of President Thomas Jefferson

White House hostess at times. Her son James Madison Randolph was the first child born in the White House.

After President Jefferson's retirement in 1809, Martha Randolph and her family lived with him at Monticello until his death in 1826.

A view of Monticello, the Jeffersons' Virginia estate

DOLLEY PAYNE TODD MADISON
1768–1849

James Madison Administration, 1809–1817

Dolley Payne was born to Quaker parents, John Payne and Mary Coles Payne, in Guilford County, North Carolina, on May 20, 1768. She was brought up on her father's plantation in Virginia in the strict discipline of the Society of Friends (the Quakers), always wearing plain gray dresses. But Dolley's Grandmother Coles, who was not a Quaker, introduced her to elegant food and clothes.

In 1783 Dolley's father freed his slaves and moved the family to Philadelphia. When his new laundry starch business failed, Mrs. Payne opened a boarding house, which Dolley helped run. At twenty-one, Dolley married a Quaker lawyer, John Todd, Jr., and had two children. Tragically, only three years later, Mr. Todd and one of their babies died in a yellow fever epidemic.

The widow Todd was unusually pretty, and she had a sunny, friendly nature in spite of the sadness of her husband's and child's deaths. In May 1794 James Madison,

A drawing of Dolley Madison saving the Declaration of Independence during the War of 1812

congressman from Virginia, began courting her. Mr. Madison's friends George and Martha Washington tried to convince Mrs. Todd to accept him, but Dolley Todd was not sure that she wanted to marry "the great little Madison," as she called him. He was seventeen years older, and an Episcopalian rather than a Quaker.

But finally Dolley Todd and James Madison were married on September 15, 1794, at the Virginia estate of her sister and brother-in-law, Lucy and George Steptoe Washington (a nephew of the president). Mrs. Madison was disavowed by the Quakers, and she happily took up a life that included fine clothes and lavish entertaining.

A depiction of the burning of Washington, D.C., by the British in the War of 1812

In 1801 James Madison was appointed Thomas Jefferson's secretary of state, and the Madisons moved to the new capital, Washington, D.C. President Jefferson, a widower, depended on Mrs. Madison to act as hostess for him. Her dinners and parties were so stylish that she was dubbed "the Queen of Washington City." Europeans as well as Americans copied Mrs. Madison's fashions in clothes, such as the silk turban.

When James Madison ran for president in 1808, Dolley Madison accompanied him on the campaign trail, winning many friends for her serious, scholarly husband with her charm and tact. It was obvious to others that the Madisons' marriage was close and loving. As the president's wife, Mrs. Madison was called "Lady Presidentess." She never took much interest in

politics, but she was fiercely patriotic, giving parties during the War of 1812 to celebrate American victories.

In August 1814, when the British were about to invade Washington, President Madison insisted his wife leave for Virginia immediately. But Dolley Madison took the time to pack a wagon with valuables, such as a famous portrait of George Washington, and important papers, including the Declaration of Independence. She escaped the city just ahead of the British troops.

In 1818 the Madisons retired to Montpelier, their estate in Virginia, where Mrs. Madison continued to enjoy entertaining. After Mr. Madison's death in 1836, however, she was forced to sell Montpelier to pay off the gambling debts of her son, John Payne Todd. (Dolley and James Madison never had children of their own.)

The Father of the Constitution, President James Madison, and Dolley Madison

Almost seventy years old and poor, she was still spirited and healthy when she returned to Washington. Dolley Madison was welcomed as a national heroine. She was awarded a small pension, and lived in Washington until her death on July 12, 1849, at the age of eighty-one.

An undated portrait of Elizabeth Monroe; Elizabeth was called "La belle Américaine" (the beautiful American) during her time in France.

$\mathcal{E}$LIZABETH KORTRIGHT MONROE
1768–1830

James Monroe Administration, 1817–1825

On June 30, 1768, Elizabeth Kortright was born in New York City, the daughter of Hannah Aspinwall Kortright and Lawrence Kortright. Her father, an officer in the British Army and a wealthy merchant, lost much of his fortune in the Revolution. Not much is known about Elizabeth's early life, but by the time she met Virginia lawyer James Monroe she was tall and beautiful and carried herself with the social poise of an aristocrat. Elizabeth and James married in February 1786, when she was not yet eighteen.

Mr. Monroe progressed rapidly from member of the Continental Congress, to United States senator, to minister to France and England, to governor of Virginia. Meanwhile, the Monroes had three children, two daughters (Eliza and Maria) and a son who died as a baby. For Mrs. Monroe the happiest period of their married life was the years in France. French manners and style suited her aristocratic tastes. Besides, America was so popular in France that when the Monroes entered a theater, the orchestra would play "Yankee Doodle" in their honor. And Mrs. Monroe was hailed as *"La belle Américaine."*

During the bloodiest stage of the French Revolution when many members of the French nobility were being killed, Elizabeth

Madame de Lafayette, wife of Marquis de Lafayette

Monroe became something of a heroine for saving the life of Madame de Lafayette, wife of the Marquis de Lafayette who had so gallantly aided the American Revolution. On the day Madame de Lafayette was due to be executed, Mrs. Monroe pointedly paid her a call in prison. The Revolutionary government took the hint and let Lafayette's wife go, to please their American allies.

In 1817, the Monroes moved into the White House. Washington society thought Mrs. Monroe was aloof and inhospitable, a disappointing replacement for popular Dolley Madison. Because she was not in good health during President Monroe's two terms, Mrs. Monroe cut back severely on official entertaining and turned over some of the social planning to her daughter Eliza Monroe Hay.

Elizabeth Monroe also ended the custom that the president's wife must spend afternoons racing around Washington in her carriage — not to actually visit, but to leave her card in the front hall of all the ladies who had called on her. With more states joining the Union all the time, the number of congressmen's wives expecting to receive a card from the president's wife was growing alarmingly. However, Washington ladies felt snubbed by Mrs. Monroe, and they boycotted her White House receptions for a time.

The Monroes' home in Oak Hill, Virginia

In spite of ill health, Mrs. Monroe managed to redecorate the White House with elegant furnishings imported from France. But after President Monroe's retirement, her health declined even more. She died five years later, on September 23, 1830, at Oak Hill, their estate in Virginia.

An engraving of Louisa Adams

$\mathcal{L}$OUISA JOHNSON ADAMS
1775–1852

John Quincy Adams Administration, 1825–1829

The only First Lady to be born outside the United States was Louisa Catherine Johnson. She was born in London, England, on February 12, 1775. Her father, Joshua Johnson, was American, a prosperous Maryland merchant. Her mother, Catherine Nuth Johnson, was English. The Johnsons spent the years of the American Revolution in France, where Louisa attended a convent school and learned to speak French. After the war, the family returned to London. Louisa, the second of eight children, sang and played the piano and the harp quite well, and loved to read and write poetry.

Louisa met John Quincy Adams, a young diplomat and the son of John and Abigail Adams, in London in 1795. They were married there on July 26, 1797, when she was twenty-two and he was thirty. That same year Mr. Adams was appointed United States minister to Berlin, where they spent the next four years.

Louisa Adams was sensitive and impulsive, while John Quincy Adams was cold and controlling, expecting his wife to obey him without question. They quarreled over everything from rouge (he forbade her to wear it) to how to treat the children (she felt he was too harsh). Mr. Adams neglected her for his work and, with one pregnancy after another, Louisa Adams's health was often poor. Only three of their children, George, John II, and Charles Francis, survived to adulthood.

When the Adamses moved to the United States in 1801, Louisa Adams felt foreign and unwelcome. Abigail Adams (Louisa's mother-in-law) was especially critical of her daughter-in-law. Louisa Adams liked Washington, D.C., better than Massachusetts, and she had finally started to adjust when President James Madison appointed John Quincy Adams minister to Russia. Without consulting his wife, Mr. Adams arranged for their two older sons, George and John, to remain in the United States to attend school and for the rest of the family to move to Russia.

The years in Russia were miserable for Mrs. Adams. The weather was brutally cold, her health was bad, they didn't have enough money, and she missed her older sons. Finally, in 1814, John Quincy Adams, already in Belgium to negotiate the treaty ending the War of 1812, sent word to his wife to leave St. Petersburg and meet him

dential race against Andrew Jackson. However, they did not enjoy the four years in the White House. John Quincy Adams's presidency was extremely trying, and Mrs. Adams was often ill and depressed.

In 1830 Mr. Adams was elected congressman from Massachusetts. During the next several years in Washington, the Adamses both became increasingly involved in the movement to abolish slavery.

Louisa Adams at age 21

John Quincy Adams

in Paris. Louisa Adams set out on a thousand-mile journey across Europe with her young son, Charles, her maid, and an unreliable Russian escort. Reaching France, they were almost pulled out of the carriage and killed by Napoleon's troops, but Mrs. Adams managed to convince the soldiers that they were Americans.

Mr. Adams and his parents were impressed with his wife's courage, and Louisa Adams's marriage improved. In 1824, she helped her husband win the close presi-

When Mr. Adams discovered his mother's letters written to her husband in 1776, he and Mrs. Adams were both deeply moved by the way Abigail Adams had spoken out against slavery and for women's rights.

On February 21, 1848, John Quincy Adams suffered a massive stroke. He died two days later without regaining consciousness. Grief-stricken, Louisa Adams died in Washington four years later, on May 15, 1852. She is buried next to her husband in Quincy, Massachusetts.

A watercolor depicting Rachel and Andrew Jackson

Rachel Donelson Robards Jackson
1767–1828

Andrew Jackson Administration, 1829–1837

Rachel Donelson was born in Virginia on June 15, 1767, to Rachel Stockley Donelson and Colonel John Donelson, a surveyor and a member of the Virginia House of Burgesses. The family followed the frontier, moving to Tennessee when Rachel was twelve, and later to Kentucky. There, as a lively, sociable girl of seventeen,

Rachel met and married Lewis Robards.

Captain Robards was a jealous, bad-tempered husband. In a fit of rage, he sent his wife home to her mother, now a widow with a boardinghouse near Nashville, Tennessee. One of the boarders was a tall, lean, reckless young lawyer named Andrew Jackson, and he and Rachel fell in love. When Lewis Robards showed up to claim his wife, the two men seemed likely to kill each other, but Rachel was persuaded to return to Kentucky with her husband.

Rachel Robards finally gave up on her marriage and fled to New Orleans. Later she heard with relief that Lewis Robards had legally divorced her, and in August 1791 she joyfully married Andrew Jackson in New Orleans. Two years later, however, the Jacksons were horrified to learn that Mr. Robards had just *now* divorced his wife in a Kentucky court. After some agonizing, the Jacksons married a second time, in Nashville, on January 17, 1794.

They settled down on the Hermitage, their plantation near Nashville. Mrs. Jackson became fervently religious. Rachel and Andrew Jackson had no children of their own, but they adopted one of her brother's sons, naming him Andrew Jackson, Jr. They also treated another nephew, Andrew Jackson Donelson, like their own son.

While Mr. Jackson was away from home, following his career in politics and the army, the Jacksons exchanged passionate letters. Mrs. Jackson managed their plantation well, to her husband's admiration, but she hated his absences and longed for Mr. Jackson to quit public life.

In 1828, when Andrew Jackson ran for president, his enemies dragged up the old scandal about their marriage. One of the milder attacks referred to the Jacksons as "a convicted adultress and her paramour husband."

Because she had been protected from the worst of the campaign against her, Rachel Jackson did not realize how vicious

A portrait of Rachel Jackson

the attacks had been until after Andrew Jackson had won the election. Reading the nasty accusations in a political pamphlet, Mrs. Jackson, now sixty-two and a devout churchgoer, was devastated. Shortly afterward, she became seriously ill. She died at home on December 22, 1828.

Ten thousand people came to the Hermitage to attend Rachel Jackson's funeral on Christmas Eve, at which Andrew Jackson wept bitterly. He was always convinced that his enemies had killed his wife with the grief and humiliation she suffered from their slander.

Hannah Van Buren died before her husband became president.

HANNAH HOES VAN BUREN
1783–1819

Martin Van Buren Administration, 1837–1841

Born on March 8, 1783, in the little Dutch town of Kinderhook, New York, Hannah Hoes was the daughter of Maria Quackenboss Hoes and John Dircksen Hoes, a Dutch farmer. She grew up in Kinderhook, as did her distant cousin Martin Van Buren, and they attended the same village school. On February 21, 1807, Hannah and Martin, now a lawyer, were married in Catskill, New York, at the home of Hannah's sister. She was twenty-three and he was twenty-four.

The Van Burens' marriage, apparently a happy one, lasted for twelve years. They spoke Dutch at home, and neither of them completely lost their Dutch accent when speaking English. They had five sons: Abraham, John, Martin Jr., Smith

Thompson, and a child who died as a baby. A niece later remembered Mrs. Van Buren's "modest, even timid manner . . . and her loving, gentle disposition."

When the Van Burens were living in Albany, Hannah Van Buren spoke up for a project to teach street waifs to read. And just before she died of tuberculosis on February 5, 1819, she asked that the money which customarily would be spent on gifts to the pallbearers at her funeral "be given to the poor."

Angelica Van Buren, the Van Burens' daughter-in-law

Martin Van Buren never remarried, and in 1837 his four grown sons moved into the White House with him. To this household of eligible bachelors Dolley Madison soon introduced Angelica Singleton, her young and beautiful cousin by marriage. Angelica, from a prominent South Carolina family, had been educated at Madame Greland's school in Philadelphia. She had refined manners and an aristocratic air. Abraham, the eldest Van Buren son, fell in love with her, and they were married in November 1838.

Angelica Van Buren began serving as the president's hostess, impressing the public with her elegance, poise, and graciousness. She sometimes received guests at the White House seated on a dais, like a queen. Sadly, during her stay in the White House she lost a child, a baby girl.

After President Van Buren retired in 1841, Abraham and Angelica Van Buren settled in New York City. Martin Van Buren died at his estate in Kinderhook on July 24, 1862, and he was buried beside his wife in the village cemetery.

President Van Buren was known for his refined taste.

Anna Harrison, dressed in mourning for her husband,
William Henry Harrison

ANNA TUTHILL SYMMES HARRISON
1775–1864

William Henry Harrison
Administration, 1841

Anna Symmes was born in Flatbrook, New Jersey, on July 25, 1775 — the year the American Revolution broke out. Her father was John Cleves Symmes, a New Jersey judge. Her mother, Anna Tuthill Symmes, died shortly after she was born. When Anna was only a few years old, her father, then a colonel in the Continental Army, disguised himself as a Redcoat and smuggled her through British lines to her grandparents on Long Island.

Growing up with her well-to-do grandparents, Anna received an excellent education at Clinton Academy in Eastham, Long Island, and at Isabella Graham's school for girls in New York City. But in 1794, when she was nineteen, she left the civilized East behind and traveled with her father to the 500,000 acres of untamed frontier land he had bought at North Bend, on the Ohio River.

Only a few months later, while visiting her older sister in Lexington, Kentucky, Anna met Lieutenant William Henry Harrison, who was then twenty-two. They fell in love immediately. Judge Symmes forbade Anna to see William, not wanting her to suffer the harsh life of a frontier officer's wife. However, on November 25, 1795, Anna defied her father and was secretly married to William in North Bend, Ohio, by a justice of the peace.

Anna Harrison was happy in her new life, even though she missed her husband, who was away much of the time in the army. She helped run their successful farm at North Bend and put her fine education to use by schooling their children, and the neighbors' as well. The Harrisons had ten

William Henry Harrison only served as president for one month.

children: Elizabeth, John Cleves, Lucy, William Jr., John, Scott Benjamin, Mary, Carter, Anna, and a baby who did not survive.

Five of the children were born at Vincennes, Indiana, during Mr. Harrison's term as governor of the Indiana Territory

before the War of 1812. At the outbreak of the war, Anna Harrison returned to North Bend. There she led a happy life centered around family, farm, and church for the next twenty-eight years.

In 1840, William Harrison was elected president. Mrs. Harrison, sixty-five, had wanted him to stay with her in retirement on their beloved farm. She was not very well that winter, and therefore she did not make the long and difficult trip from Ohio to Washington, D.C., to attend President Harrison's inauguration in March. Several weeks later, when she was preparing to leave for Washington, Anna Harrison received shocking news: Her husband had died of pneumonia on April 4, 1841.

Mrs. Harrison continued to live at the farm in North Bend until the house burned down in 1858. She then went to stay with her only surviving child, John Scott Harrison, on his nearby farm. Even at the age of eighty-eight, Anna Harrison's mind stayed clear and lively; her doctor told her grandchildren, "I never met a more entertaining person than your grandmother." She died on February 25, 1864, and she was buried beside her husband at North Bend.

A drawing depicting the death of William Henry Harrison

Letitia Tyler took no part in the social activities of the White House.

LETITIA CHRISTIAN TYLER
1790–1842

John Tyler Administration, 1841–1845

Letitia Christian was born at Cedar Grove, her family's plantation near Richmond, Virginia, on November 12, 1790. Her father was Colonel Robert Christian; her mother, Mary Brown Christian. As a planter's daughter, Letitia was taught the skills of managing a large household and making other people's lives comfortable and pleasant. She grew up to be a lovely but very quiet, shy, and religious (Episcopalian) young woman.

During her long engagement to John Tyler, the young law student sent her elaborate love letters. "Whether I float or sink in the stream of fortune," he wrote her shortly before their marriage, " . . . I shall never cease to love you." Although their engagement lasted five years, Letitia was always so "reserved and modest," as John told his friends, that he did not dare to kiss her hand until a few weeks before the wedding.

On March 29, 1813, Letitia (twenty-two) and John (it was his twenty-third birthday) were married at Letitia's home, Cedar Grove. Throughout their twenty-nine-year marriage, Mrs. Tyler seems to have been happy taking care of her family and running the household. The Tylers had seven children who survived to adulthood: Mary, Robert, John Jr., Letitia, Elizabeth, Alice, and Tazewell.

Mr. Tyler progressed in his political career, aided by his wife's wealth and social standing, but Mrs. Tyler avoided public life. She made only one visit to Washington, D.C., during the nine years her husband was senator from Virginia. She became increasingly religious and read nothing except the Bible and her prayer book.

In 1838 Letitia Tyler suffered a paralyzing stroke, and from then on she was con-

fined to either her bed or an invalid's chair. When John Tyler became president in April 1841, after President William Harrison's death, Mrs. Tyler finally came to Washington, but she took no part in the social activities of the White House.

Luckily Priscilla Cooper Tyler, the wife of the Tylers' son Robert, was willing and able to serve as President Tyler's hostess. Priscilla, who was beautiful and intelligent, had been an actress before her marriage. She enjoyed being in the public eye and

John Tyler was vice-president until the death of William Harrison.

welcoming such celebrities as authors Washington Irving and Charles Dickens to the White House. Letitia Tyler still oversaw the running of the household from the living quarters on the second floor, but only once, at her third daughter Elizabeth's wedding to William N. Waller in January 1842, did she come downstairs for a social occasion.

Soon afterward, on September 10, 1842, Letitia Tyler died of a second stroke. Mourned by her family as "the most entirely unselfish person you can imagine," in the words of Priscilla Tyler, she was buried at her birthplace, Cedar Grove.

The Tylers' daughter-in-law, Priscilla Cooper Tyler

"The most beautiful woman of the age and...most accomplished," President Tyler said of his new bride, Julia Tyler.

 JULIA GARDINER TYLER
1820–1889

John Tyler Administration, 1841–1845

Julia Gardiner was born in 1820 on Gardiner's Island, New York, to Juliana McLachlan Gardiner and David Gardiner, a rich landowner. Both her parents were from wealthy and prominent New York families. After attending a fashionable finishing school in New York City, Julia made her social debut in Saratoga Springs, New York, and then toured Europe with her family.

The Gardiners went to Washington, D.C., for the winter social season of 1842–43. With her beauty, poise, and flirtatious manner, Julia Gardiner was soon the most admired belle in the capital. President Tyler himself, just out of mourning for his first wife, fell in love with her. At first, Julia was not very interested in the president's courtship; she even read his flowery love letters to her family.

But then, in February 1844, her father died in an accidental explosion on the steam frigate *Princeton*, during a presidential cruise. In the time John Tyler comforted the distraught Julia, she began to see him in a different light. On June 26, 1844, Julia Gardiner and John Tyler were married in a private ceremony in New York City.

There was a great deal of public excitement, since John Tyler was the first president to be married while in office. President Tyler's sons seem to have accepted their young new stepmother, but his daughters, who had not even been told about the wedding beforehand, were shocked and upset.

Once in the White House, Julia Tyler managed to cram a series of dazzling receptions, balls, and dinners into less than a year. President Tyler was proud of his socially brilliant young wife, and she in turn ardently supported his policies, such as the principle of states' rights.

After President James Polk's inaugura-tion in 1845, the Tylers retired to Sherwood Forest, their Virginia plantation. They had seven children: David Gardiner, John Alexander, Julia, Lachlan, Lyon Gardiner, Robert Fitzwater, and Pearl. Julia Tyler adopted her husband's Southern loyalties, vigorously defending the Confederacy to her Northern relatives.

In January 1862, Mr. Tyler went to Richmond to serve in the Confederate Congress. Soon after he left, Mrs. Tyler was frightened by a dream that he was ill, and rushed to Richmond. Two days later, on January 18, to his wife's grief, John Tyler was dead of a stroke.

Julia Tyler moved back to New York, but she was estranged from her family because of her Southern sympathies. Impoverished by the depression of the 1870's, she applied to Congress for a pension as a president's widow, but it was not granted until 1880.

Meanwhile, Mrs. Tyler returned to Virginia. On July 10, 1889, she died in Richmond of a stroke. She is buried beside President Tyler in Richmond, in the presidents' section of the Hollywood Cemetery.

The explosion of a navy gun in 1844 accidentally killed two of President Tyler's cabinet officers and Julia Gardiner's father.

As First Lady, Sarah Polk hosted the first Thanksgiving dinner at the White House.

SARAH CHILDRESS POLK
1803–1891

James K. Polk Administration, 1845–1849

On September 4, 1803, Sarah Childress was born near Murfreesboro, Tennessee, to a wealthy planter, Captain Joel Childress, and Elizabeth Whitsitt Childress. Sarah was extremely well-educated for a girl of her time, attending first a boarding school in Nashville and then the Moravian Female Academy in Salem, North Carolina. She was always an avid reader, and fascinated with politics.

Sarah met James Knox Polk, a hard-driving, ambitious young lawyer, in 1821. He proposed to her in 1823 — at the urging of Andrew Jackson, so the story goes. In Jackson's opinion, Sarah Childress was the perfect wife (wealthy, intelligent, good-looking) to help James's political career. The wedding took place on New Year's Day, 1824, when she was twenty and he was twenty-eight.

That fall Mrs. Polk encouraged her husband to campaign for United States congressman. When he won, she was delighted to move to Washington and plunge into national politics. Mr. Polk counted on her to keep up with political issues, read his speeches, and advise him. A charming, tactful, and lively woman, she also helped her husband gain a place in important Washington social circles.

Since the Polks had no children, Mrs. Polk could devote all her time to working as her husband's private secretary and advisor. In 1839, when James Polk ran for governor of Tennessee, she acted as his campaign manager, arranging his schedule and sending out campaign literature.

As the result of a bitter election race in 1844, James Polk was an unpopular

Sarah Polk   *President James Polk*

president, but everyone seemed to like and admire Mrs. Polk. She entertained in the White House with confidence and pleasure, although more sedately than Julia Tyler had. A devout Presbyterian, Mrs. Polk did not allow card-playing or dancing in the White House. People stopped paying

Sunday calls on the Polks, for fear they would be invited to attend church with them.

Sarah and James Polk both worked hard during his term as president, so much so that by the spring of 1849 President Polk was worn out. The Polks decided to tour the Eastern seaboard before retiring to

A humorous depiction of the Polk inauguration reception

their new home in Nashville, but during the tour Mr. Polk became seriously ill, possibly of cholera picked up in New Orleans. He died on June 15, 1849.

Mourning her loss, Sarah Polk turned Polk Place, their Nashville mansion, into a sort of museum for President Polk. During the Civil War, the Polks' home was considered neutral territory, and Mrs. Polk entertained Union officers as well as Confederates. She felt that as a former president's wife, she should rise above her Southern sympathies.

Mrs. Polk died on August 14, 1891, at the age of eighty-seven. She was buried beside her husband at Nashville.

Margaret Taylor chose not to serve as White House hostess.

Margaret Mackall Smith Taylor

1788–1852

Zachary Taylor Administration, 1849–1850

Margaret "Peggy" Mackall Smith was born on September 21, 1788, in Calvert County, Maryland, to Walter Smith and Ann Mackall Smith. Her father was a well-to-do planter and a former officer in the Revolutionary War, and Margaret was brought up to be a proper young lady. There is no authentic surviving portrait of her, but she was said to be slender and dark-haired.

Visiting a sister near Louisville, Kentucky, in 1809, Margaret met Lieutenant Zachary Taylor, while he was home on leave from Fort Pickering, Tennessee. Although Margaret was painfully shy, they quickly fell in love. They were married on June 21, 1810, at her sister's log house, when Margaret was twenty-one and Zachary was twenty-five.

Although Mrs. Taylor had grown up in refined plantation society, she followed her husband without hesitation from one isolated and primitive fort on the Western frontier to another. She made homes for her family in tents and log cabins, in outposts from Fort Snelling, Minnesota, to Tampa, Florida. Furthermore, good-natured Margaret Taylor did all she could to make the harsh garrison life easier for others. She visited sick and wounded soldiers, cheered up the other officers' wives, and educated the children.

The Taylors had six children, but two of the girls died young, in 1820, of a "bilious fever" which also injured Mrs. Taylor's health. Four children lived to grow up: Ann, Sarah, Mary Elizabeth ("Betty"), and Richard. In 1835 Sarah eloped with Lieutenant Jefferson Davis, the future president of the Confederacy, then serving under Colonel Taylor.

By 1848 Zachary Taylor was a popular Mexican War hero, and the Whig Party nominated him for president. Filled with dismay, Margaret Taylor prayed with all her heart that he would not be elected. In good spirits she had borne almost forty years of hardship and danger on the frontier, but she dreaded the public splendor of the White House.

Once in Washington, Mrs. Taylor asked her daughter Betty, now married to President Taylor's secretary, Lieutenant Colonel William W.S. Bliss, to perform the duties of White House hostess. Margaret Taylor received friends privately upstairs in the White House due to her ill health. She did not leave the mansion except to attend church services.

After the lengthy ceremony for laying the cornerstone of the Washington Monument on July 4, 1850, President Taylor became seriously ill. He died a few days afterward on July 9. Overcome with grief,

Margaret and Zachary Taylor's daughter, Betty Taylor Bliss

Mrs. Taylor left the White House, never even to speak of it again.

Margaret Taylor lived the last years of her life with her son-in-law and daughter, William and Betty Bliss, near Pascagoula,

Zachary Taylor died in office.

Mississippi. There she died on August 18, 1852, at the age of sixty-four. She was buried next to her husband in Louisville, Kentucky.

Abigail Fillmore personally selected the books for the White House library.

ABIGAIL POWERS FILLMORE
1798–1853

Millard Fillmore Administration, 1850–1853

Abigail Powers was born in Stillwater, New York, on March 13, 1798, to Lemuel Powers, a prominent Baptist minister, and Abigail Newland Powers. Her father died soon after Abigail's birth, leaving *little* money but *many* books. Her mother decided to take Abigail and her brother to Cayuga County, on the frontier, where they had relatives and it would be less expensive to live. There the mother used the library to educate Abigail and her brother at home.

At sixteen, Abigail became a teacher. At nineteen, teaching at an academy in New Hope, she met Millard Fillmore — a tall, good-looking farm boy who was two years younger than she was. For a few months he was her pupil, and she was impressed with his ambition and determination. He was inspired by her passionate dedication to learning and her respect for him.

The next year, Abigail and Millard became engaged. She encouraged him for the eight long years of their engagement while he

Mary "Abby" Fillmore, the Fillmores' daughter, often acted as White House hostess.

finished his education, including law school and the bar exams. In February 1826 they were married in Moravia, New York, at the home of her brother, Judge Powers.

Abigail Fillmore continued teaching until her son, Millard Powers Fillmore, was born in 1828, making her the first First Lady to hold a job after getting married. In 1829 Mr. Fillmore began serving as a representative in the New York State Legislature, and by 1830 his law practice was doing well enough that the Fillmores were able to move to a comfortable home in Buffalo. Their second child, Mary Abigail, was born there in 1832.

When Millard Fillmore served in the United States Congress (1833–35 and 1837–43) Abigail Fillmore went to Washington with him. Mr. and Mrs. Fillmore often discussed public affairs, and sometimes he would ask her advice on an issue.

Millard Fillmore was elected Zachary Taylor's vice president and, upon President Taylor's death in July 1850, he became president. Mrs. Fillmore was not eager to do the official entertaining expected of a president's wife, and she often asked her daughter "Abby" to fill in as White House hostess.

Upon moving into the White House, Abigail Fillmore was shocked to find that there was no proper library. She asked the president to have Congress appropriate money for one and personally selected the books for the library in the Oval Room upstairs.

President Fillmore sometimes talked over the business of his office with his wife, but he did not take her best piece of advice — not to sign the Fugitive Slave Act. This decision ruined Millard Fillmore's chances for re-election in 1852.

After attending Franklin Pierce's inauguration on the raw, cold day of March 4, 1853, Abigail Fillmore came down with pneumonia. Only a few weeks later, she died in the Willard Hotel in Washington, at the age of fifty-five. She was buried in Buffalo, New York.

Millard Fillmore was the last president elected by the Whig Party.

Jane Pierce in a portrait with her beloved son, Bennie

JANE APPLETON PIERCE
1806–1863

Franklin Pierce Administration, 1853–1857

Born in Hampton, New Hampshire, on March 12, 1806, Jane Appleton was the daughter of Elizabeth Means Appleton and the Reverend Jesse Appleton, a Congregationalist minister and president of Bowdoin College. Her father died when Jane was thirteen, and her mother took her to live with her well-to-do, religious grandparents in Amherst, New Hampshire. She grew up to be a delicate and pious young woman.

In 1826 Jane met Franklin Pierce, who was studying law in nearby Northampton, Massachusetts, and then in Amherst, New Hampshire. A handsome, outgoing, ambitious young man, Franklin wanted to make his name in politics. In spite of their opposite personalities, Jane and Franklin fell deeply in love. After an eight-year egagement, they were married on November 19,

1834, in Jane's grandparents' Amherst home, by Jane's brother-in-law, the Reverend Silas Aiken.

Mr. Pierce was already a representative in Congress when they married, but Jane never approved of his political career. Most of the time she stayed at their home in Hillsborough, New Hampshire, rather than share her husband's public life. She was not happy for him in 1836, when he was elected to the United States Senate.

The Pierces' first child, named Franklin after his father, died when he was only a few days old. Too frail to do household chores, Jane Pierce devoted herself to religion. She held daily prayer services and Bible readings at home and attended the Congregational church on Sundays.

*President Franklin Pierce,
nicknamed "Handsome Frank"*

For his wife's sake, Franklin Pierce gave up his Senate seat in 1842, and the Pierces moved to Concord, New Hampshire. After their second child, Frank, died of typhus at the age of four, Jane poured all her love and energy into the upbringing of their third son, Benjamin ("Bennie").

Franklin Pierce served in the army dur-ing the Mexican War, but in 1848 he returned home to Concord. For the next few years, Mr. Pierce practiced law and Mrs. Pierce thankfully enjoyed the company of her husband and their young son.

In 1852 Franklin Pierce ran for president on the Democratic ticket, although he had assured Mrs. Pierce that he would not run. And in spite of his wife's and son's fervent prayers that he would lose, he won the November election. Jane Pierce felt betrayed. Then, in January 1853, when the three Pierces were returning home from Boston by train, there was an accident. Eleven-year-old Bennie was killed.

Jane Pierce never recovered from the death of her beloved Bennie. In the White

*A portrait of Jane Pierce, who never
recovered from her son's death*

House, she stayed upstairs in seclusion most of the time, writing letters to her dead son.

When Franklin Pierce's term was up in March 1857, the Pierces began a three-year tour of the West Indies and Europe, hoping in vain to improve Jane Pierce's health. She died of tuberculosis in Andover, Massachusetts, on December 2, 1863, and she was buried in Concord, New Hampshire, near Bennie's grave.

*Harriet Lane,
Buchanan's
orphaned niece,
served as official
White House
hostess during
his presidency.*

HARRIET LANE JOHNSTON
1830–1903

*James Buchanan Administration,
1857–1861*

Harriet Lane was born in Franklin County, Pennsylvania, on May 9, 1830, the daughter of Elliott Lane, a prosperous merchant, and Jane Buchanan Lane. When Harriet was orphaned at the age of eleven, she asked that James Buchanan, her favorite uncle, become her guardian. He was delighted to take on his "mischievous romp of a niece."

Mr. Buchanan supervised Harriet's education in private schools and at the Visitation Convent in Georgetown. She grew from a tomboy into a still lively but exceptionally poised young woman. James

Buchanan, then secretary of state to President James Polk, was proud to introduce her to Washington society.

In 1854 Harriet "Hal" Lane joined her uncle in London, where he was the United States minister to Great Britain. Pretty, charming Miss Lane became a favorite of Queen Victoria, who gave her the rank of ambassador's wife. Mr. Buchanan warned her not to let her head be turned with all the attention she was receiving from suitors, but Harriet Lane seems to have been a levelheaded young woman, despite her love of fine clothes, parties, and flirting.

When James Buchanan became president in March 1857 (he was the only president who never married), his twenty-six-year-old niece moved into the White House with him and, with confidence, took over the

James Buchanan was the first and only bachelor president.

role of official hostess. Washington society was delighted after the dismal years of the Franklin Pierce administration, and they called her the "Democratic Queen." The song "Listen to the Mockingbird" was written in her honor, and a steamboat was named after her, as were many baby girls.

The feelings between North and South were already bitter before President Buchanan took office, and Harriet Lane had to bring all her social training and skill to bear, just to work out the seating at official dinners — to keep enemies apart and yet give each guest the proper place due to his or her rank. Toward the end of President Buchanan's term, however, no social skill could prevent the country from falling apart.

In March 1861, with the beginning of the Civil War only weeks away, an exhausted James Buchanan thankfully retired to Wheatland, his estate near Lancaster, Pennsylvania. Harriet Lane lived with him there until, at the age of almost thirty-six, she married a Baltimore banker, Henry Elliott Johnston.

The Johnstons had two sons, but neither of them lived to adulthood. After eighteen years of marriage, Harriet Johnston's husband also died. She moved back to Washington in order to be near her friends; she enjoyed traveling and adding to her art collection.

Upon her death in 1903, Harriet Lane Johnston bequeathed that impressive collection to the Smithsonian Institution. Most of her estate went to found a home for invalid children at Johns Hopkins Hospital in Baltimore, and her name lives on in the Harriet Lane Outpatient Clinic there.

A portrait of Mary Lincoln by the famous Civil War photographer, Matthew Brady

MARY TODD LINCOLN
1818–1882

Abraham Lincoln Administration, 1861–1865

Mary Todd was born in Lexington, Kentucky, on December 13, 1818, to Elizabeth Parker Todd and Robert Smith Todd, a prosperous banker. Mary's mother died when Mary was six, after which her father remarried. A bright, vivacious girl, Mary attended the best schools, where she studied French, music, art, and drama.

As a young woman Mary Todd was pretty, witty, and popular, although high-strung. In 1839 she went to live with her married sister, Elizabeth Edwards, in Springfield, Illinois. There, at a dance, she met a tall, awkward, self-taught country lawyer named Abraham Lincoln. Mary's family did not think Abraham worthy of her, but Mary and Abraham were power-fully attracted to each other. After an on-again, off-again courtship, they were married on November 4, 1842, at Mary's sister's house in Springfield.

The Lincolns settled in Springfield, where Mr. Lincoln practiced law. Although they were opposites in temperament, Abraham Lincoln appreciated his wife's quick wit and liveliness, bearing patiently with her outbursts of temper and her sometimes irrational fears. The Lincolns had four sons — Robert, Edward ("Eddy," who died at the age of four), William ("Willie"), and Thomas ("Tad") — and they doted on their children.

With his wife's encouragement, Abraham Lincoln was elected to the United States House of Representatives in 1846. In 1855 he ran unsuccessfully for the United States Senate, and ran in 1858 against Stephen A. Douglas and lost again. But finally, in 1860, he was elected president. Mrs. Lincoln re-joiced in his victory, believing that Mr.

Lincoln could unite the now divided nation. She was also looking forward to reigning over Washington society.

A few weeks after President Lincoln's inauguration, the Civil War broke out. Abraham Lincoln was unpopular in the

Mary Lincoln with sons Willie (left) and Tad (right) in 1860

North as well as the South, and so was Mrs. Lincoln. She was unfairly accused of being a Southern sympathizer because her half-brothers were fighting for the Confederacy. She could not even give parties without being criticized in the press for extravagance in wartime, although she did overspend her budget for refurbishing the White House, causing President Lincoln to lose his usual good temper.

In February 1862 the Lincolns' son Willie, eleven years old, died of typhoid fever. Almost insane with grief, Mary Lincoln feared that her older son, Robert, might die in the war. She absolutely refused to allow him to serve in the Union Army, bringing further criticism on the president.

By early 1865 Mary Lincoln was finally recovering from Willie's death, but she still suffered from headaches and haunting fears. However, the Lincolns' lives seemed to be taking a turn for the better. Newly re-elected, President Lincoln was finally popular, for the war was won and the country reunited. On the evening of April 14, the Lincolns attended a light-hearted play at Ford's Theater—and there a Southern sympathizer, John Wilkes Booth, shot the president. He died the next day.

Mary Lincoln was too distraught to attend her husband's funeral, and lay in bed for weeks afterward. After she left the White House, she was terrified of poverty, for she had run up enormous debts during the White House years. Congress did not appropriate a pension for her until 1870.

Mary Lincoln's one comfort was her son, Tad, but in 1871 Tad, only eighteen, died of tuberculosis. His mother's mental state was further unbalanced. In 1875 her remaining son Robert had her declared insane.

Raging against Robert as "a wicked monster," Mrs. Lincoln managed to get herself released from the mental hospital. She died in Springfield, Illinois, at her sister Elizabeth Edwards's house, on July 15, 1882. Mary Todd Lincoln was buried next to her husband in the Oak Ridge Cemetery in Springfield.

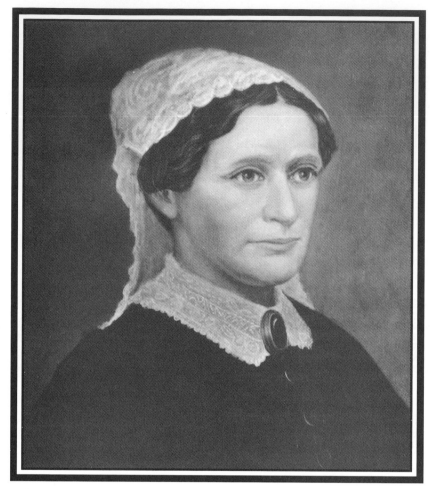

Eliza Johnson taught her husband how to read and write.

ELIZA McCARDLE JOHNSON
1810–1876

*Andrew Johnson Administration,
1865–1869*

Eliza McCardle was born on October 4, 1810, in Leesburg, Tennessee. She was the only child of a shoemaker, John McCardle, and Sarah Phillips McCardle. Eliza's father died when she was still a little child, and she was brought up by her mother in Greeneville, Tennessee.

When Eliza was sixteen, she and some friends watched a penniless tailor's apprentice move into town. Eliza liked the young man, Andrew Johnson, right away, and he felt the same way about her. Less than a year later, on May 17, 1827, they were married.

When he was first married, Andrew Johnson was ambitious, but he barely knew how to read. His young wife, who had attended Rhea Academy in

Greeneville, tutored him in reading and taught him writing and arithmetic.

With Mrs. Johnson's encouragement, Mr. Johnson advanced quickly in politics, from

Martha Patterson, the Johnsons' daughter, acted as hostess due to her mother's poor health.

mayor of Greeneville in 1830 to United States senator in 1857. In the meantime, the Johnsons had five children: Martha, Charles, Mary, Robert, and Andrew, Jr. Since Andrew Johnson's political career took him away from Greeneville much of the time, Eliza Johnson managed the family business as well as the household.

In 1862 President Lincoln appointed Mr. Johnson military governor of Tennessee. While Andrew Johnson was in the temporary state capital of Nashville, Jefferson Davis forced all Union supporters, including Mrs. Johnson and her family in Greeneville, to leave the Confederate-held portion of the state. Eliza Johnson was already ill with tuberculosis, and the forced move further damaged her health.

By the time Andrew Johnson was sworn in as president in April 1865, Eliza Johnson was an invalid. Moving into a room on the second floor of the White House, she quietly enjoyed her children and grandchildren, while her daughter Martha Johnson Patterson acted as White House hostess.

President Johnson, who opposed the harsh policies that the North wanted to inflict on the defeated South, was hated and scorned. On February 24, 1868, he was actually impeached, and subsequently he was tried by the Senate for alleged "high crimes and misdemeanors." In spite of her frail health, Eliza Johnson supported her husband through the trial. When he was acquitted on May 16, she exclaimed, "I knew it!"

In 1869, after Ulysses S. Grant's inauguration, the Johnsons returned to

Because of his boyhood occupation, President Johnson was known as the "Tennessee Tailor."

Greeneville. Andrew Johnson ran unsuccessful campaigns for the Senate and House of Representatives, but finally was elected to the Senate in 1874. His wife rejoiced at his triumphant return to Washington after near-disgrace in the presidency.

But sadly, on July 31, 1875, Andrew Johnson died of a stroke. Six months afterward, Eliza Johnson died of tuberculosis at her daughter Martha Patterson's house. The Johnsons were buried side by side near Greeneville.

JULIA DENT GRANT
1826–1902

Ulysses S. Grant Administration, 1869–1877

Julia Boggs Dent was born on January 26, 1826, to Ellen Wrenshall Dent and Colonel Frederick Dent, on their plantation near St. Louis. Julia attended the Misses Mauros' boarding school in St. Louis, where she did especially well in art and voice. She was plain and a little cross-eyed, but well-liked by boys as well as girls for her outgoing, fun-loving personality.

In 1844 Julia met Lieutenant Ulysses S. Grant, a classmate of her brother's at West Point. "Ulys," as she called him, was handsome but shy. Julia was strongly drawn to the quiet young soldier, and he fell deeply in love with warmhearted Julia.

Julia's father, Colonel Dent, thought Lieutenant Grant was too poor to marry his daughter. As for the Grants, they disapproved of Julia because her parents were slaveholders. Still, on August 22, 1848, after a four-year engagement, Julia and Ulysses were married at the Dents' home in St. Louis. The Grants did not attend the wedding, but eventually they came to accept Julia, who did not share her father's commitment to slavery.

Whenever Julia and Ulysses Grant were together, they were happy. Julia Grant followed her husband from one military post to another, then lived with her parents

Julia Grant held impressive White House receptions.

for two years while he was stationed in the West. Julia and Ulysses Grant had four children: Frederick, Ulysses Jr., Ellen, and Jesse.

In 1854 Mr. and Mrs. Grant returned to their farm near St. Louis. He was unsuccessful at running the farm and failed at other business ventures, but his wife never lost faith in him. During the Civil War he had the chance to prove his military brilliance, ultimately becoming commander of all the Union armies. Mrs. Grant often joined her husband in the field. She had strong opinions about what the general ought to do, and sometimes he followed her advice.

In 1868, Civil War hero General Grant was elected president, to Julia Grant's joy.

Ulysses and Julia Grant with family and friends at Mount McGregor, New York

She thought her husband deserved the high office, and she intended to enjoy her own position as the president's wife.

President Grant was popular, and Mrs. Grant was praised rather than criticized for launching a series of extravagant balls, receptions, and dinners. Because of Julia Grant's warm, friendly nature, the White House receptions were open to working-class people as well as foreign royalty and the richest Americans. In 1874 the Grants' daughter Nellie was married in the White House, in the grandest style, to Algernon Sartoris, an Englishman.

To his wife's deep disappointment, President Grant refused to run for a third term. However, she was soon consoled when the Grants set off on a world tour in May 1877. For the next few years the Grants enjoyed living more quietly

together, until they lost all their money in a bad investment in 1884. Much worse, General Grant learned that he had cancer of the throat.

Ulysses S. Grant died on July 23, 1885, at Mount McGregor, New York. Mrs. Grant was overwhelmed with grief. Of small consolation was the fact that the autobiography General Grant had just completed sold well and left her well provided for.

Julia Grant settled in Washington, where she enjoyed the company of her children and grandchildren and friends, and wrote her memoirs. On December 14, 1902, Mrs. Grant died; she was buried beside her husband in the imposing mausoleum for General Grant in New York City.

Friends at West Point joked that Ulysses S. Grant's initials stood for "Uncle Sam."

*Lucy Hayes
in a greenhouse
with two of her
children*

LUCY WARE WEBB HAYES
1831–1889

*Rutherford B. Hayes Administration,
1877–1881*

Lucy Webb, the daughter of Dr. James Webb and Maria Cook Webb, was born in Chillicothe, Ohio, on August 28, 1831. Her father, a physician, died when she was two, but Lucy received an excellent education, first attending Ohio Wesleyan College and then graduating from Wesleyan Female College in Cincinnati.

While Lucy was still in college, a lawyer named Rutherford B. Hayes moved to Cincinnati. He had met Lucy a few years before, and now he began to see a great deal of her. He wrote in his diary about her "low sweet voice" and "quick spritely" intellect. On December 30, 1852, Lucy and Rutherford were married in her home in Cincinnati.

Before marriage Lucy Hayes had been sympathetic to the women's rights movement, but afterward she adopted her husband's view that women should stick to home and family. However, Mrs. Hayes was passionately antislavery, and she helped win Mr. Hayes over to this cause.

Lucy Hayes absorbed herself with their children. Three died in infancy, but five lived to grow up: Birchard, James Webb Cook, Rutherford Platt, Frances, and Scott. While Mr. Hayes went to Washington as congressman and then served three terms as governor of Ohio, Lucy Hayes was known for being gracious and sweet-natured. During the Civil War, when her husband was in command of a regiment, Mrs. Hayes visited him and his soldiers in camp and tended the sick and dying. The grateful troops nicknamed her "Mother Lucy."

Rutherford Hayes became president in March 1877, and most people praised the new First Lady. Lucy Hayes loved entertaining and did so with quiet good taste. Some complained about the lack of

A drawing of Lucy Hayes greeting a deputation of ladies in the Blue Room of the White House

alcohol at White House functions, but the anti-alcohol Women's Christian Temperance Union made Mrs. Hayes their heroine.

Many women's rights advocates hoped that Lucy Hayes, the first college graduate of the presidents' wives, would stand as an example of the "new woman," entitled to education and opportunities outside home and family. But when Susan B. Anthony and Elizabeth Cady Stanton asked Mrs. Hayes to support a bill to allow women attorneys to appear before the Supreme

A photograph of President Rutherford B. Hayes and First Lady Lucy Hayes

Court, she refused. She would not even attend commencement at the Women's Medical College of Philadelphia.

Lucy Hayes stuck to the motto that had, in her opinion, served her well for many years of married life: Never get involved in politics. Fittingly, the social climax of President Hayes's term was the celebration of their silver wedding anniversary.

In March 1881 the Hayeses retired to Spiegel Grove, their estate at Fremont, Ohio. Mrs. Hayes contentedly settled into a round of church activities, visiting with her children and grandchildren, and traveling with her husband. Eight years later she died of a stroke on June 25, 1889. President and Mrs. Hayes are buried together at Spiegel Grove.

A portrait of Lucretia Garfield

LUCRETIA RUDOLPH GARFIELD
1832–1918

James A. Garfield Administration, 1881

Lucretia Rudolph was born on April 19, 1832, in Hiram, Ohio, to Arabella Mason Rudolph and Zebulon Rudolph. Her father was a farmer and one of the founders of a Disciples of Christ school, the Eclectic Institute. Bright and eager to learn, Lucretia received a good education at the Geauga Seminary in Chester, Ohio, and then at the Eclectic Institute.

James Garfield attended school with Lucretia ("Crete"), and for a long time he was not sure they were suited. He was social and affectionate, while Lucretia was reserved and cool. However, Lucretia and James had in common their membership in the Disciples of Christ Church, their devotion to education, and their enjoyment of lectures and concerts.

In 1854 James went off to Williams College in Massachusetts to complete his last two undergraduate years, while Lucretia taught school in Ohio. She was tormented as James changed his mind several times about whether or not he

James and Lucretia Garfield with their family

really loved her. But finally on November 11, 1858, they were married in a quiet ceremony at Lucretia's father's house in Hiram.

During their first few years of marriage, Mr. Garfield was often away from home in the Ohio State Senate and then in the Union Army during the Civil War. Mrs. Garfield was miserable much of the time, doubting that her husband loved her. In fact, he called their marriage "a great mistake."

Then the years of separation ended, in 1863, with Mr. Garfield's election to Congress. Their eight children were born, five of whom survived: Harry, James Rudolph, Mary ("Mollie"), Irvin, and Abram. During their time in Washington, the Garfields grew to enjoy each other's company, traveling, socializing, attending cultural events, or just reading and playing cards.

As a young woman, Lucretia Rudolph had believed that women should have equal opportunities with men in education and careers. After marriage, however, she came to share her husband's stand against even giving women the vote. Mrs. Garfield almost worshiped her husband, and she thought of him as a future president years before he ran in 1880. Needless to say, she was elated when he won the election.

To her frustration, Lucretia Garfield became ill with malaria within a few weeks after the inauguration. By May she was so sick that she went off to a resort to recover. On July 2, 1881, James Garfield was shot and badly wounded by a mentally unstable office-seeker, Charles J. Guiteau. Lucretia Garfield rushed home to Washington, determined to nurse her husband back to health. However, to her bitter grief, President Garfield died on September 19, 1881.

Lucretia Garfield preparing food for her ill husband

Lucretia Garfield and her family retired to Lawnfield, their estate in Mentor, Ohio. She worked on records of President Garfield's life, read literature, wrote, and enjoyed watching her grandchildren grow up. On March 14, 1918, she died in Pasadena, California. She was buried next to her husband in the Lake View Cemetery in Cleveland.

Chester Arthur had a bouquet of flowers placed daily next to this siver-framed photograph of Ellen "Nell" Arthur.

ELLEN LEWIS HERNDON ARTHUR
1837–1880

Chester A. Arthur Administration, 1881–1885

On August 30, 1837, Ellen Herndon was born into an old Southern family in Culpeper Court House, Virginia. Her parents were Elizabeth Hansbrough Herndon and William Lewis Herndon, a naval officer. When Ellen (called "Nell") was a girl, the family moved to Washington, D.C., where her father helped establish the Naval Observatory. Nell loved music and had a pleasing contralto voice; she sang in the choir at St. John's Episcopal Church on Lafayette Square.

While in New York in 1856 Nell was introduced to a tall, good-looking lawyer, Chester Arthur, by her cousin Dabney Herndon. In spite of their differences — he was the up-and-coming son of a Baptist minister, Republican, and several years older — Nell and Chester fell in love. When Nell's father died in 1857, Chester

Arthur helped the Herndon family through the crisis, even managing Mrs. Herndon's financial affairs.

On October 25, 1859, Nell and Chester were married in Calvary Episcopal Church in New York City. For the next few years, during the Civil War, there was a strain in the family. All the Herndons, including Nell Herndon Arthur, sympathized with the Southern cause, while Chester Arthur served in the New York militia on the Union side. However, he still helped his wife's family as much as he could.

In the post-Civil War years, Mr. Arthur's law practice prospered, and during President Grant's administration he was collector of the port of New York. The Arthurs and their children, Chester Jr., and Ellen ("Nell"), enjoyed high living, spending and entertaining in the finest style. Mrs. Arthur continued to sing, giving recitals to friends and performing for charity fund-raisers.

During President Rutherford B. Hayes's administration, Mr. Arthur was accused of corruption, and in 1878 he was fired from his post as collector. There was some tension between Mr. and Mrs. Arthur over the time he spent away from her, socializing with friends and advancing his political career. Then, ten months before Chester Arthur's election as vice president in November 1880, Ellen Arthur caught a cold from waiting outside for a carriage after a concert. Two days later, she was critically ill with pneumonia. On January 10, 1881, she died at the age of forty-two.

Chester Arthur was overcome with grief and remorse. In his wife's memory he gave a stained glass window to St. John's Episcopal Church in Washington, placed so that he could see the window from the White House. In spite of his grief over his wife's death, President Arthur entertained with elegance. His youngest sister, Mary

President Chester Alan Arthur

Mary Arthur McElroy: youngest sister of President Arthur and ranking lady of his admin- istration

McElroy, served as hostess during his term in office.

By the time he left office in 1885, President Arthur was seriously ill with Bright's disease, a kidney ailment. He died on November 18, 1886, in New York City, and was buried next to his wife in Rural Cemetery, Albany, New York.

Frances Clevland around the time of her wedding to Grover Cleveland; they were the only first couple to be married in the White House.

FRANCES FOLSOM CLEVELAND
1864–1947

Grover Cleveland Administrations, 1885–1889; 1893–1897

Born in Buffalo, New York, on July 21, 1864, Frances Folsom was the daughter of Emma Cornelia Harmon Folsom and Oscar Folsom, a lawyer. Soon after birth she was introduced to her father's law partner, Grover Cleveland, a bachelor, who gave her a baby carriage.

When Frances was eleven, her father died in a horse-and-buggy accident. Grover Cleveland became the administrator of his partner's estate and an unofficial guardian —"Uncle Cleve"—to Frances. By the time she went off to Wells College in Aurora, New York, she was a beautiful, socially poised young woman, and he asked her mother's permission to write her.

Soon Mr. Cleveland, now the governor of New York, was sending Frances flowers, too, and they were both in love. But he waited until August 1885, when she had graduated from college and he was president, to propose marriage.

Grover Cleveland was the first Democratic president since the Civil War.

The press suspected President Cleveland of planning a marriage, but they assumed his intended bride was his partner's widow. It was not until late May 1886, when Frances and her mother returned from a trip to Europe, that Grover Cleveland announced he would marry Frances Folsom on June 2. He was the only president to be married in the White House; the few guests included his cabinet.

Frances Cleveland was the youngest First Lady ever; she married Grover Cleveland at age twenty-one. She charmed the press, Washington society, and even President Cleveland's political enemies. She herself never took any interest in politics, but she tried to keep her husband from overworking.

Mrs. Cleveland's popularity as First Lady had something to do with President Cleveland's political success. He lost the election of 1888, but he was re-elected president in 1892 — with campaign posters featuring Frances Cleveland's picture between Grover Cleveland and his running mate, Adlai Ewing Stevenson.

The Clevelands had five children: Ruth, Esther (the first child born to a president in the White House), Marion, Richard Folsom, and Francis Grover. In 1897, when President Cleveland's second term was up, they retired to Princeton, New Jersey. Mr. Cleveland became a trustee of Princeton University, and Mrs. Cleveland enjoyed entertaining faculty and students.

But then Grover Cleveland's health began to fail, and he was sometimes in bed for weeks on end with rheumatism. In 1904 the Clevelands were desolated by the death of their twelve-year-old daughter, Ruthie, of diphtheria. Then, on June 24, 1908, Grover Cleveland died of a heart attack.

Frances Cleveland stayed in Princeton, and five years later she married Thomas J. Preston, Jr., a professor of archeology. On October 29, 1947, at the age of eighty-three, Frances Folsom Cleveland Preston died in her sleep during a visit to her son Richard in Baltimore. She was buried next to President Cleveland in Princeton.

The Cleveland family; the Baby Ruth candy bar was named for their daughter, Ruth.

First Lady Caroline Harrison in 1889

CAROLINE SCOTT HARRISON
1832–1892

Benjamin Harrison Administration, 1889–1893

Caroline Lavinia Scott was born in Oxford, Ohio, on October 1, 1832, to Mary Neal Scott and the Reverend John W. Scott, a Presbyterian minister. Her father founded the Oxford Female Institute, where Caroline ("Carrie") was educated. She was a lively, outgoing girl, talented in music and art.

When Carrie was seventeen she met Ben Harrison, a student of her father's at Farmers' College in Cincinnati. After Ben transferred to Miami University of Ohio, near Oxford, they began seeing each other all the time. Carrie sometimes persuaded serious, reserved Ben to take her dancing, although their strict Presbyterian church forbade it.

Carrie and Ben became secretly engaged in 1852. The next year, she graduated from the Oxford Female Institute and began teaching music. At first they planned to put off marriage until Ben had his law degree. But they couldn't stand the separation, and finally they were married by Carrie's father on October 20, 1853, at her home in Oxford.

First the Harrisons lived on Benjamin Harrison's father's farm, to save money, while he finished his law studies. Then they moved to Indianapolis, Indiana, where it took a few years for Mr. Harrison to establish his law practice. Meanwhile, they had two children, Russell and Mary ("Mamie").

During the Civil War, Mr. Harrison served in the Union Army. He missed Mrs. Harrison greatly, and he sent her letters full of remorse that he had neglected her for his work. After the war, they did spend more time together. Mrs. Harrison kept up her artistic interests, painting water colors and teaching china-painting classes.

In 1881, the same year Mr. Harrison began his term in the United States Senate, Caroline Harrison suffered a bad fall, and her health was delicate after that. Still, in 1889, when Benjamin Harrison became president, she eagerly took up her duties as First Lady.

President Benjamin Harrison

Mrs. Harrison wanted to enlarge the White House, which was much too small for the Harrisons and their extended family: Mrs. Harrison's father; her widowed niece, Mary Scott Lord Dimmick; and the Harrisons' daughter Mary S. Harrison McKee, her husband, and their two children. However, Congress provided only enough money for repairs and modernization, such as the installation of electric lights. The Harrisons were glad for the renovations, but afraid of electricity; they refused to touch the switches.

Caroline Harrison with her father, her daughter, and two grandchildren

In 1890 Caroline Harrison helped found the Daughters of the American Revolution. She also helped raise funds for the Johns Hopkins Medical School, on the condition that they admit women. She established the historic White House china collection and put up the first White House Christmas tree.

By the time President Harrison ran for re-election in 1892, Mrs. Harrison was seriously ill with tuberculosis, and he cut down on his campaigning in order to be with her. On October 25, 1892, at the age of sixty, Caroline Harrison died in the White House. She was buried in Indianapolis.

Ida McKinley was the first president's wife to have worked in a profession other than teaching.

IDA SAXTON MCKINLEY
1847–1907

William McKinley Administration, 1897–1901

Born in Canton, Ohio, on June 8, 1847, Ida Saxton was the elder daughter of Catherine Dewalt Saxton and James A. Saxton, a well-to-do banker. Ida attended a first-rate school, the Brook Hall Seminary in Media, Pennsylvania, and then finished off her education with a European tour.

Lovely and vivacious, Ida did not marry right away, but began working as a cashier at her father's bank. Then she met William McKinley, a young lawyer, at a picnic, and before long they were in love. On January 25, 1871, when she was twenty-three and he was twenty-seven, they were married at the First Presbyterian Church in Canton.

The newlyweds set up housekeeing in the home in Canton that Ida's father bought for them. Their first daughter, Katherine ("Katie"), was born on Christmas Day, 1871, and they doted on her and on each other. Then, in 1873, Mrs. McKinley's mother died. Mrs. McKinley was devastated by this loss. Then a few months later, her new baby Ida died.

From then on, Ida McKinley suffered from severe headaches and epileptic seizures. She developed phlebitis, which partly crippled her. Worst of all, her first daughter, Katie, died from typhoid fever in 1876, when she was only four.

In spite of his political ambition, William McKinley devoted himself to making Ida McKinley happy. The same year that Katie died, he was elected to Congress. His invalid wife moved to Washington with him, and they went for carriage drives, to

The ladies of the cabinet of President McKinley

the theater, sometimes to White House dinners. By herself, Mrs. McKinley often did needlework.

In 1892 Mr. McKinley was elected governor of Ohio, and the McKinleys took up residence in a hotel facing the capitol. Every afternoon at three o'clock, Governor McKinley would wave a handkerchief out his office window, and Mrs. McKinley would wave back from the hotel.

When William McKinley became president in 1897, Ida McKinley was happy and proud, and determined to do her part as First Lady in spite of her ill health. In

reception lines, she greeted guests while seated on a blue velvet chair. At official dinners Mrs. McKinley always sat next to the president, and if she began to have a

President McKinley seated next to his wife Ida

seizure, President McKinley would quickly spread a handkerchief over her face so that guests would not be alarmed by her contortions.

In September 1901, after William McKinley's re-election, the McKinleys traveled to the Pan-American Exposition in Buffalo, New York. There, on September 6, President McKinley was shot and wounded by an unemployed anarchist, Leon F. Czolgosz. Mrs. McKinley took the news bravely and hoped for her husband's recovery. But infection set in, and he died on September 14.

Ida McKinley returned to Canton, Ohio. Her health grew worse, but she visited her husband's grave almost every day. She died on May 26, 1907, at the age of fifty-nine, and she was buried next to President McKinley and their two little daughters in Canton.

Edith Roosevelt the year her husband became president

EDITH KERMIT CAROW ROOSEVELT

1861–1948

Theodore Roosevelt Administration, 1901–1909

Edith Carow was born in Norwich, Connecticut, on August 6, 1861. The daughter of Gertrude Elizabeth Tyler Carow and Charles Carow, a merchant, Edith grew up in high society. The Carows' house in New York City was next to the Roosevelts', and Edith was friendly with Theodore as well as his sisters. She completed her education at Miss Comstock's school.

Edith and Theodore enjoyed books and nature together, in New York and at the Roosevelt summer house in Oyster Bay, Long Island. By the time Theodore went off to Harvard in 1876, they were sweethearts. Then they quarreled, and in 1880 Theodore married a Boston girl instead, Alice Hathaway Lee.

But Alice Roosevelt died in 1884, shortly after their baby, Alice, was born. In the fall of 1885, Edith Carow and Theodore Roosevelt met once more at his sister

Anna's house, and soon they were in love again. On December 2, 1886, they were married in London, where Edith's family was living. Edith was twenty-five and Theodore was twenty-eight.

After a honeymoon in Europe, the Roosevelts settled down in Oyster Bay. Besides Alice, Mr. Roosevelt's daughter by his first marriage, they had five children: Theodore Jr., Kermit, Ethel Carow, Archibald Bulloch, and Quentin. While Mr. Roosevelt pursued his political career, Mrs.

Teddy and Edith Roosevelt with Richard Derby in 1915

Roosevelt managed the finances and kept discipline in the family. The parents both loved their family life, and Mrs. Roosevelt joined in the family games enthusiastically.

In 1900, when Theodore Roosevelt was governor of New York, Mrs. Roosevelt advised him not to run for vice president with William McKinley. However, he did, and in September 1901 President McKinley was shot, making Mr. Roosevelt president.

As First Lady, Mrs. Roosevelt calmly managed a hectic social schedule of receptions, teas, and dinners, to say nothing of the wedding of Alice to Nicholas Longworth in 1906 and Ethel's social debut in 1908. She kept a firm rein on her husband's boyish enthusiasm and made sure he got enough rest. Mrs. Roosevelt also supervised the addition of the East and West Wings to the White House.

In 1909, Edith Roosevelt was happy to retire to Oyster Bay. She enjoyed private life there until World War I, when the Roosevelts' youngest son, Quentin, was killed in battle in 1918. Mr. and Mrs. Roosevelt were heartbroken. Theodore Roosevelt's health failed, and the next year he died of a coronary embolism.

After that Edith Roosevelt lived quietly, reading, traveling, doing charity work, and enjoying her family. Increasingly

The Roosevelts: (left to right) Quentin, Theodore, Theodore Jr., Archie, Kermit, Edith, and Ethel

conservative politically, she did not support her husband's cousin Franklin Roosevelt for president in 1932.

On September 30, 1948, Edith Roosevelt died at Oyster Bay at the age of eighty-seven. She was buried there next to her husband.

A photo of Helen Taft at the time of William Taft's presidency

HELEN HERRON TAFT
1861–1943

William H. Taft Administration, 1909–1913

Helen Herron was born June 2, 1861, in Cincinnati, Ohio. Her mother was Harriet Collins Herron; her father, Judge John W. Herron, was Rutherford B. Hayes's law partner. Helen ("Nellie") was fascinated by history and politics and, after a visit to President Hayes's White House at age 17, she decided she was going to live there some day. Nellie graduated from the Cincinnati College of Music, studied at Miami University, and then taught school.

In the winter of 1879, Nellie met Will Taft, a likeable young lawyer, at a bobsledding party. Will was not only attracted to Nellie, but he also valued her intelligence and drive. After a long courtship, they were finally engaged in May 1885 and married on June 19, 1886, in Nellie's parents' home in Cincinnati.

After a honeymoon in Europe, the Tafts settled down in Cincinnati. Mr. Taft had a law practice and hoped to become a judge

— and someday a Supreme Court Justice. But Mrs. Taft kept steering him toward national politics. They had three children: Robert, Helen, and Charles.

In January 1900 President William McKinley appointed William Taft governor-general of the Philippine Islands. Mrs. Taft leaped at this chance to advance Mr. Taft's political career. In the Philippines she thrived on the adventure—from weathering typhoons to reigning in the governor's palace as a colonial queen.

When Theodore Roosevelt became president, he offered to appoint Mr. Taft a justice of the Supreme Court, but Mrs. Taft adamantly refused to agree to this. However, in 1904 her husband accepted the position of secretary of war. In Washington, she began cultivating Republican contacts, intent on getting Mr. Taft

Helen Taft with two of her three children: Robert, 2, and Helen, 6 months

nominated for president in 1908. With Mrs. Taft urging him on, he won both the nomination and the election.

Helen Taft basked in the glory of the inauguration in 1909, the first president's wife to ride from the Capitol to the White House with her husband. But sorrowfully, that May she suffered a stroke, and she could not walk or talk normally again for almost a year. Yet she recovered to launch her daughter Helen's debut and to give a huge silver anniversary party in 1911. Mrs. Taft's most enduring achievement in Washington was the planting of three thousand cherry trees.

Helen Herron Taft as a young girl

In March 1913 the Tafts left the White House, to William Taft's relief and Helen Taft's sorrow. They lived more quietly in Connecticut, where Mr. Taft taught law at Yale. Then Mr. Taft's lifetime dream came true in 1921, when President Warren Harding appointed him to the Supreme Court. Mrs. Taft was thrilled to return to Washington. Several years later, in March 1930, William Taft died of heart disease.

Helen Taft continued to live in Washington, proud of her children: Robert, a United States senator; Helen, Dean of Bryn Mawr College; and Charles, civic leader of Cincinnati. She died on May 22, 1943, at the age of eighty-one, and she was buried beside her husband in Arlington National Cemetery.

ℰLLEN AXSON WILSON
1860–1914

Woodrow Wilson Administration, 1913–1921

Ellen Louise Axson was born in Savannah, Georgia, on May 15, 1860. Her mother was Margaret Hoyt Axson; her father, the Reverend Samuel E. Axson, was a Presbyterian minister. At the Female Seminary in Rome, Georgia, Ellen studied literature, music, and art. She was a particularly gifted painter.

It was in Rome, in April 1883, that Ellen met Woodrow Wilson, a lawyer from Atlanta visiting his cousin. Woodrow was smitten at once with Ellen's "splendid, mischievous laughing eyes," and he discovered that she was intelligent and cultured as well. By September they were engaged, although they delayed marriage while he finished his graduate work and she studied painting in New York City.

Ellen was twenty-five and Woodrow twenty-eight when they were married at her grandfather's home in Savannah on June 24, 1885, by two ministers: her grandfather and Woodrow's father. The newlyweds moved to Pennsylvania, where Woodrow Wilson taught at Bryn Mawr College. As he moved on to Wesleyan University, in Connecticut, and then to Princeton University, Ellen Wilson devoted all her intelligence, talents, and quiet charm to making her husband happy and

The first First Lady of the Wilson administration, Ellen Wilson

furthering his career.

Mrs. Wilson proofread Mr. Wilson's articles and books, and she coached him in the subjects she knew well, such as art and literature. She ran the household, making ends meet on a college professor's skimpy salary. And she educated their three daughters, Margaret, Jessie, and Eleanor.

After Woodrow Wilson became governor of New Jersey in 1911, he began thinking of running for president in 1912. During his bid for the Democratic nomination,

Mrs. Wilson helped him rehearse his speeches, courted key politicians, and gave him political advice. She believed her husband was destined for greatness, and she was thrilled when he was elected president.

Although Mrs. Wilson did not care about the glory of being First Lady, she entertained with well-bred grace. Even

A photograph of Ellen Wilson, circa 1910

with a hectic schedule, she found time to paint in a studio in the White House, and she remained her husband's constant companion and supporter, going over his speeches, discussing the issues, and advising him.

Ellen Wilson also took an interest in the working conditions of people in the federal government departments, and she insisted that rest rooms be installed for the women. Appalled by the alleys of substandard housing where black people lived in

The Wilsons and their three daughters: Margaret, Jessie, and Eleanor

Washington, she lobbied Congress for a remedial bill.

In the spring of 1914 Mrs. Wilson became ill with Bright's disease, a then-fatal kidney ailment. When she died on August 6, 1914, Woodrow Wilson was grief-stricken. Ellen Wilson was buried with her parents in Rome, Georgia.

Edith Wilson was devoted to the war effort.

EDITH BOLLING GALT WILSON
1872–1961

Woodrow Wilson Administration, 1913–1921

Edith Bolling was born in Wytheville, Virginia, on October 15, 1872, to Sallie White Bolling and William Holcombe Bolling, a circuit court judge. The Bollings were an old Virginia family, and on her mother's side Edith was a descendant of Pocahontas. Edith was educated in private girls' schools in Virginia. In 1896 she married Norman Galt, a jeweler in Washington, D.C. After he died in 1908, Edith Galt ran the jewelry store.

One day in April 1915, Mrs. Galt visited a friend in the White House, President Wilson's cousin Helen Woodrow Bones. She accidentally met the president, and they were immediately drawn to one another. Woodrow Wilson was still in mourning for his first wife, but he was quite taken with handsome, lively Edith Galt. By September, they were engaged.

The president's advisors were afraid that marrying again so soon would damage his political career, and they tried to discourage the match. In spite of their efforts, Edith Bolling Galt and Woodrow Wilson were married on December 18, 1915, in a small private ceremony in her home in Washington. She was forty-three and he fifty-eight.

Like Ellen Wilson, the second Mrs. Wilson was devoted to her husband. President Wilson discussed everything with her and even brought her into special sessions with his advisors about the progress of World War I. Besides acting as White House hostess, Edith Wilson ran the household and the president's financial affairs.

After the end of World War I in November 1918, when President Wilson

Edith Wilson (left) in Geneva, en route to the League of Nations meeting

went to Paris to work on the peace treaty, Mrs. Wilson accompanied him, proud of her husband and his dream of creating a world without war. But she was concerned that he was pushing himself too hard.

Back in the United States that summer, President Wilson continued to work unre-

lentingly to get the Senate to accept the peace treaty and the League of Nations. But on October 2, 1919, he suffered a stroke that left him partly paralyzed.

Many people, including Mrs. Wilson, felt the president should resign. But President Wilson's doctors persuaded her to keep his administration going and protect him from strain. Therefore, Edith Wilson allowed no one but herself to see the president. She reviewed all official papers, showed him the ones that needed immediate attention, and communicated his decisions. She was accused, especially by the Republican opposition, of grabbing power, but she adamantly denied that she made any decisions herself.

President Wilson finally recovered enough to appear in public, but he was never really well again. In March 1921 the Wilsons retired to their house in Washington, where he died in February 1924.

Edith Wilson continued to live in Washington. A loyal and respected member of the Democratic Party, she supported Franklin Roosevelt in his campaign for the presidency. In 1939, she published her own account of her husband's administration, *My Memoir*.

When the United States joined the United Nations in 1945, Mrs. Wilson rejoiced at this fulfillment of Woodrow Wilson's dream. Her last public appearance was in 1961, riding in President John Kennedy's inaugural parade. She died later that year on her husband's birthday, December 28, at the age of eighty-nine, and she was buried beside him on the grounds of the National Cathedral in Washington.

Florence Harding worked as the circulation manager for her husband's newspaper, the Daily Star, *and contributed greatly to their financial success.*

FLORENCE KLING DE WOLFE HARDING
1860–1924

Warren G. Harding Administration, 1921–1923

On August 15, 1860, Florence Mabel Kling was born in Marion, Ohio. Her mother was Louisa Bouton Kling; her father, Amos Kling, a banker, was the richest man in Marion. Florence ("Flossie") went to local schools and then studied music at the Cincinnati Conservatory of Music. Intelligent and headstrong, at nineteen she eloped with Henry De Wolfe, a coal dealer's son.

When Henry De Wolfe deserted Florence and their baby, she returned to Marion. There she supported herself by giving piano lessons. She divorced Mr. De Wolfe, and finally she had no alternative but to give her son, Marshall, to her parents to raise.

In 1890 Florence met Warren Harding,

owner of a Marion newspaper, the *Daily Star*. She was irresistibly attracted to handsome, easygoing Warren. Her father was against the match, but Florence and Warren were married on July 8, 1891. She was thirty, he was twenty-five.

Mrs. Harding began to help with the circulation department of the *Daily Star*. She was soon in charge of circulation, then of advertising. Because the Hardings had no children, Florence Harding traveled often with her husband. She even poured drinks for him and his friends at poker parties.

With Mrs. Harding running the household and to some extent the newspaper, Mr. Harding became involved in Republican politics. Mrs. Harding advised him, encouraged him, and rewrote his speeches. She was delighted to see him progress from state senator to United States senator by 1914.

Florence Harding enjoyed living in Washington as a senator's wife, hobnobbing with important people. In 1920, when some Republicans wanted to nominate Warren Harding for president, he tried to refuse, but Mrs. Harding persuaded him to run.

Mr. Harding won the election by a wide margin, and Florence Harding was delighted and proud. She suffered from a kidney ailment, but as First Lady she was determined not to skimp on entertaining. Her specialty was garden parties for the World War I veterans, who loved Mrs. Harding's folksy style. In private, the Hardings continued to throw poker parties, serving liquor as usual although Prohibition was the law.

Warren Harding was a very popular president, but his adminisration was corrupt. When the Teapot Dome scandal finally became public, President Harding sank into depression. Florence Harding, not well herself, was consumed with anxiety.

For a healing change of scene, the Hardings set off on a trip to the West Coast and Alaska in June 1923. But on the

Florence Harding fixing the lapel of President Harding's suit jacket

way the president suffered a heart attack, and on August 2 he died in San Francisco of a stroke.

With her husband gone, Florence Harding lost her remarkable determination. She went home to Marion, and on November 21, 1924, she died of kidney disease. She was buried beside President Harding in Marion, Ohio.

Grace Coolidge poses on the steps of the White House in an evening gown.

GRACE GOODHUE COOLIDGE

1879–1957

Calvin Coolidge Administration, 1923–1929

Grace Anna Goodhue was born in Burlington, Vermont, on January 3, 1879, the only child of Lemira Barrett Goodhue and Andrew Isaachar Goodhue, a steamboat inspector. A naturally cheerful and outgoing girl, Grace was educated at the University of Vermont. In 1902 she moved to Northampton, Massachusetts, to teach at the Clark School for the Deaf.

One day in 1904 Grace glimpsed a man shaving through a window of the boardinghouse next door—wearing only long underwear and a derby hat. Hearing her laugh, the man — Calvin Coolidge, a lawyer — was determined to meet her. Grace was sunny-tempered and sociable, while Cal was stern and silent, but they hit it off. They were married in the Goodhues' home in Burlington on October 4, 1905, when she was twenty-six and he was thirty-three.

The Coolidges made their home in Northampton, where Mr. Coolidge was elected mayor in 1910. Mrs. Coolidge brought up their two boys, John and Calvin, Jr., even playing baseball with them. Their father was often away; as

"Silent Cal" Coolidge with Grace and family

lieutenant governor and then governor of Massachusetts, he rented a room in Boston and came home on the weekends.

Mr. Coolidge never discussed his work with his wife, and she never tried to influence his decisions. But he was finicky, and he criticized her cooking and her household accounts and generally told her what to do. Although he was a penny-pincher, he spent large amounts of money on her clothes.

In 1921 Calvin Coolidge became Warren Harding's vice president, and the Coolidges moved to Washington. Grace Coolidge, such a contrast to "Silent Cal," was liked immediately in the capital for her gaiety and warmth.

When Warren Harding died in 1923 and Mr. Coolidge became president, Mrs. Coolidge was not eager to take on the job of First Lady. But she entertained with seeming ease and genuine friendliness. For Grace Coolidge the hardest thing about the White House years must have been the death of their son Calvin, Jr., from blood poisoning, in 1924.

In 1928 President Coolidge announced, without telling his wife first, that he would not run for re-election. Mrs. Coolidge took the surprise with good humor. Happy to return to Northampton, she worked for the Red Cross and served on the board of trustees for the Clark School for the Deaf.

In January 1933, Calvin Coolidge died suddenly at home of a coronary thrombosis, or a blood clot in the heart. Grace Coolidge felt lost for a time, but she continued to live a full life. She traveled to Europe, took her first airplane ride, spent time with her son John and his family, and followed baseball as a loyal Boston Red Sox fan. During World War II, she helped to bring refugee children to the United States.

On July 8, 1957, Mrs. Coolidge died in Northampton of a heart attack. She was buried beside Calvin Coolidge in Plymouth, Vermont.

Grace and Calvin Coolidge campaigning

Lou Hoover and the president often spoke Chinese so that no one could eavesdrop.

*L*ou HENRY HOOVER
1874–1944

*Herbert Hoover Administration,
1929–1933*

Lou Henry was born in Waterloo, Iowa, on March 29, 1874, to Charles D. Henry, a banker, and Florence Ida Weed Henry.

When she was ten, the family moved to California. Lou loved sports and the outdoors, and her father often took her camping. After attending the San Jose Normal School, in 1894 she entered Stanford University in Palo Alto, California.

At Stanford Lou was the only female geology major; she met Herbert Hoover in the geology laboratory. They had much in common: Both were born in Iowa in the same year, both moved to California about the same time, and both enjoyed the outdoors. By the time he graduated they were serious about marriage, but Lou was determined to finish her studies, so Herbert went off to Australia as a mining engineer while she completed her education.

On February 10, 1899, Herbert and Lou were married at Lou's parents' home in Monterey, California. They honeymooned on a boat to China, where he had a new mining job.

Mrs. Hoover had the training in geology to understand the mining business, and she quickly learned Chinese. She worked with her husband, trekking to remote mining sites. In June 1900 the Boxer Rebellion broke out against foreigners in China, but Lou Hoover calmly bicycled through snipers' bullets and served tea as the Hoovers' house was shelled.

In 1901 Mr. Hoover joined a British mining firm, and during the next several years the Hoovers traveled all over the world, from Europe to Australia. They had two sons, Herbert, Jr., and Allan. Mr. Hoover became a millionaire, and the Hoovers became used to entertaining in high style.

When World War I erupted in 1914, the Hoovers devoted themselves to public service, especially efforts to provide food and clothing and hospitals in war-torn Belgium. In 1917 President Woodrow Wilson appointed Herbert Hoover as his food administrator, and the Hoovers returned to the United States. Mrs. Hoover supported her husband's food conservation programs, organizing women's groups and the Girl Scouts, of which she was the national president.

In 1921 Herbert Hoover became President Warren Harding's secretary of commerce. Mrs. Hoover now entertained almost nonstop, helping her reserved husband

President Elect Hoover and family after hearing of victory in 1928 in Palo Alto, California

to socialize with important people. She also promoted the League of Women Voters and the Campfire Girls.

Mrs. Hoover was proud and happy when Mr. Hoover won the election for president in 1928 by a wide margin. But only a few months after the Hoovers moved into the White House, the financial crash of October 1929 signaled the onset of the Great

Depression. The Hoovers cut back on their lavish lifestyle, and Mrs. Hoover gave large donations to charities. She broadcast a radio speech from the White House (a first for a First Lady), urging women to help the needy. But still, many people held President Hoover responsible for the Depression.

When Franklin Roosevelt won the election of 1932, Lou Hoover was bitterly

Herbert and Lou Hoover at a baseball game

disappointed, feeling her husband had been unfairly blamed for the Depression. However, she enjoyed their retirement in Palo Alto, California, in the Spanish-style home she had designed herself. Although she was in her sixties, she hiked and spent time with her sons and grandchildren and continued working for the Girl Scouts.

When World War II began, Mr. and Mrs. Hoover took on humanitarian projects again, spending time in New York City in their work to aid European refugees. On January 7, 1944, Mrs. Hoover suddenly collapsed and died of a heart attack. She was buried at Palo Alto, but reinterred beside her husband in West Branch, Iowa, after his death in 1964.

Eleanor Roosevelt

ELEANOR ROOSEVELT ROOSEVELT
1884–1962

Franklin D. Roosevelt Administration, 1933–1945

On October 11, 1884, Anna Eleanor Roosevelt was born in New York City to Anna Hall and Elliott Roosevelt. As Eleanor was growing up, her mother, a society beauty, was disappointed in her homely, shy daughter and favored Eleanor's two younger brothers. Eleanor adored her affectionate father, Elliott Roosevelt, but he was an alcoholic and also not at home very much. By the time Eleanor was ten, both parents had died and she was living with her strict Grandmother Hall.

When Eleanor was fifteen, she was sent to London to attend Allenswood, an excellent school. There, at last, she gained confidence and made friends. At eighteen Eleanor returned to New York for her debut. Almost six feet tall and plain, she was dreading the social whirl, but it brought her together with handsome, charming Harvard student Franklin Delano Roosevelt. He was impressed when his distant cousin

*Eleanor Roosevelt (right) and
her brother*

Eleanor took him on a tour of the tenements on the Lower East Side, where she was teaching in a settlement house.

To Eleanor's surprise, Franklin fell deeply in love with her, convinced that this idealistic young woman would help him "amount to something some day." On March 17, 1905, when he was twenty-three and she was twenty, Eleanor and Franklin were married in New York.

After the wedding, Eleanor was dominated by Franklin's mother. Sara Delano Roosevelt decided where the young couple would live, and how their children — Anna Eleanor, James, Elliott, Franklin D. Jr., and John Aspinwall — should be brought up. Under her mother-in-law's influence, Eleanor gave up her settlement house work, and she felt useless and unhappy.

In 1910 Franklin Roosevelt won a seat in the New York State Senate and moved his family to the state capital, Albany. Here Eleanor Roosevelt was introduced to the fascinating world of politics. In 1913, President Woodrow Wilson appointed Mr. Roosevelt assistant secretary of the navy.

Eleanor Roosevelt talking with Aubrey Williams, Executive Director of the National Youth Administration, and Mary Bethune, NYA Director of Negro Activities, at a conference in 1937

The Roosevelts moved to Washington, and after World War I, Eleanor Roosevelt began to get seriously involved in politics, encouraged by her husband and his secretary, Louis Howe.

In 1921, Franklin Roosevelt was stricken with polio and paralyzed. Eleanor Roosevelt not only cared for him during his illness but urged him to continue his political career. In 1928, she helped him campaign for governor of New York — and win. Governor Roosevelt could not travel, so Mrs. Roosevelt became his "eyes and ears," visiting state prisons and hospitals and reporting on how they were run.

Convinced that her husband could lead America out of the Great Depression, Mrs. Roosevelt worked hard on his successful campaign for president in 1932. In her first year as First Lady, she traveled 38,000 miles around the country, from slums in Puerto Rico to villages in Maine. She urged the president and his officials to improve federal programs, and she held her own weekly press conferences. Tireless, Mrs. Roosevelt wrote a monthly magazine column and a daily newspaper column, "My Day," and published three books of memoirs, *This Is My Story* (1937), *On My Own* (1958), and *The Autobiography of Eleanor Roosevelt* (1961).

Eleanor Roosevelt also worked to better

Franklin and Eleanor Roosevelt leaving church on Easter Sunday in Washington, D.C.

the plight of African-Americans. In 1939, she defied the prestigious Daughters of the American Revolution and arranged for the black singer Marian Anderson to perform at the Lincoln Memorial after she had been

Mrs. Roosevelt embarking on a two-and-a-half-mile trip into a coal mine

denied the stage at Constitution Hall. During World War II, she helped raise the spirits of American troops by visiting them in the war zones.

In 1945, President Roosevelt died suddenly of a cerebral hemorrhage. After his death, Eleanor Roosevelt continued to work for the goals they had shared. President Harry S. Truman sent her to the newly created United Nations, where she chaired the commission that wrote the Universal Declaration of Human Rights. She kept up her writing and lecturing, and she campaigned for Democrats running for office.

On November 7, 1962, Eleanor Roosevelt died of a rare blood disease, aplastic anemia, at the age of seventy-eight. She was buried beside her husband at Hyde Park. She had probably been one of the most loved and most hated First Ladies.

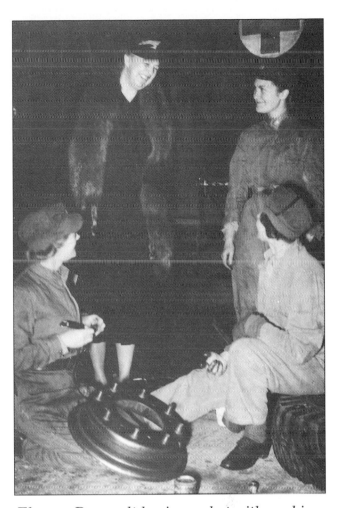

Eleanor Roosevelt having a chat with working women in 1942

Eleanor Roosevelt at an address before the United Nations in 1948

Bess and Harry Truman with their daughter, Margaret, during the rigorous whistle-stop campaign for re-election

ELIZABETH WALLACE TRUMAN
1885–1982

Harry S. Truman Administration, 1945–1953

Elizabeth Virginia Wallace was born in Independence, Missouri, on February 13, 1885, to David W. Wallace and Margaret Gates Wallace. Her mother was from a prominent Independence family; her father was a deputy county recorder. "Bess" was athletic, climbing trees and playing baseball and tennis.

When Bess was eighteen, her father, in debt and drinking heavily, killed himself. She never really got over it. Bess, her mother, and three younger brothers went to live with her grandparents, the Gateses.

Bess had met Harry Truman in Sunday School, when she was five and he was six. Harry later said it was love at first sight of her blue eyes and golden curls. They were classmates through high school, but only friends.

In 1905 Bess went off to finishing school in Kansas City. Harry, too poor to go to college, left Independence to help run his family's farm. In 1910 Harry met Bess again on a visit to Independence. He courted her for years — Bess was in no hurry to get married.

After Harry returned from fighting in France in World War I, Bess and Harry were finally married on June 28, 1919, in Trinity Episcopal Church in Independence. After the honeymoon they moved into the Gates mansion with Bess's mother.

Mrs. Truman was determined to be a full partner in her husband's work, but she shrank from public exposure. In 1934, during Harry Truman's campaign for United

States senator, she decided to appear on the platform with him, but not to make speeches or give interviews herself. In private, however, Mr. Truman always discussed everything with his wife.

After the election, Senator and Mrs. Harry Truman and their family — their daughter Margaret, born in 1924, and Bess Truman's mother — moved to Washington. Mrs. Truman worked in her husband's office, sorting mail, doing research, and helping him revise his speeches.

Bess and Margaret Truman

In 1944, when Mr. Truman was asked to run as Franklin Roosevelt's vice president, he refused at first. That might have been because Mrs. Truman was afraid that the campaign would bring up the painful fact of her father's suicide. But Mr. Truman ran in spite of this.

But shortly after President Roosevelt's inauguration in March 1945, he died. As Harry Truman was sworn in as the new president on April 12, Bess Truman stood beside him, aghast for the Roosevelt family, for the country — and for herself. Now First Lady, Mrs. Truman immediately cancelled the weekly press conferences that Mrs. Roosevelt had held.

In the first few months of Harry Truman's presidency, Mrs. Truman was distressed that he spent little time with her and no longer discussed his work. After a fierce quarrel, President Truman made her again "a full partner in all my transactions — politically and otherwise."

Bess Truman did not want her husband to run for a second term in 1948, but she accompanied him dutifully on his whistle-stop campaign as he spoke to crowds from the back platform of the train. She also sat in on planning sessions with his advisors and helped him with his speeches.

President Truman's second term, which included the Korean War and the rise of militantly anticommunist McCarthyism, was just as difficult as the first. In 1952 Mrs. Truman talked him out of a third term. She was overjoyed to escape the "Great White Jail" (the White House) and go back to Independence.

After Harry Truman's death in 1972, Bess Truman continued to live quietly in Independence, reading, following baseball, and keeping up with her daughter Margaret and Margaret's four sons. On October 18, 1982, at the age of ninety-seven, she died of heart failure — the oldest First Lady in American history. She was buried beside her husband in the courtyard of the Harry S. Truman Library in Independence.

Mamie Eisenhower boarding the presidential plane in 1958

MAMIE GENEVA DOUD EISENHOWER
1896–1979

Dwight D. Eisenhower Administration, 1953–1961

On November 14, 1896, Mamie Geneva Doud was born in Boone, Iowa, to Elivera Carlson Doud and John Sheldon Doud. Her father was so successful in the meatpacking business that he retired when Mamie was seven and took the family to Denver,

Colorado. There Mamie grew up in a big house with servants, spending winter vacations in San Antonio, Texas. She attended Miss Wolcott's finishing school in Denver. Mamie loved parties, and she went out several times a week.

In October 1915, at Fort Sam Houston near San Antonio, Mamie met Second Lieutenant Dwight Eisenhower—"Ike." She was taken with him right away, and Ike began courting her steadily. They were married at the Doud home in Denver on July 1, 1916. Mamie was nineteen, and Ike was twenty-five.

After the honeymoon, they moved into married officers' quarters at Fort Sam Houston. Only a few weeks later, Lieutenant

Mamie Eisenhower's first public appearance as First Lady Elect, at a fund-raiser for the USO

Eisenhower left his bride to go on a temporary assignment. "My country comes first and always will," he explained as he packed. "You come second."

In her own words, this was "quite a shocker," but Mamie Eisenhower adored her husband and believed he would become a great soldier. As they moved from one army post to another — twenty-seven times in thirty-seven years — she strove to help her husband in his military career. She coached him on social graces, handled the finances, and threw fabulous parties (their quarters were dubbed "Club Eisenhower").

In January 1921 the Eisenhowers' first son Doud, nicknamed "Icky," only three years old, died of scarlet fever. The Eisenhowers were devastated. It was not until the next year, at the base in the Panama Canal Zone, that they began to recover. In 1922 another son, John Sheldon Doud, was born.

After several more assignments, including a long stint in the Philippines, the Eisenhowers returned in 1941 to Fort Sam Houston. On December 7, Mrs. Eisenhower was listening to a football game on the radio when an announcer broke in with news of the Japanese attack on Pearl Harbor. During World War II, Dwight Eisenhower was overseas for more than three years, commanding the Allied forces. He and Mrs.

Mamie Eisenhower in 1943 just before the start of her first press conference

Eisenhower wrote letters often, and she busied herself with Red Cross work and kept a scrapbook of her husband's victories. But she missed him horribly. She suffered from an inner ear ailment that caused her to stumble, resulting in rumors that she was an alcoholic, but this was untrue.

After the war, General Eisenhower was an international hero. Mamie Eisenhower was not only ecstatic to have him home but bursting with pride. When he ran for president in 1952, Mrs. Eisenhower was doubtful at first, but she soon found she liked campaigning. She loved "seeing thousands and thousands of people adoring Ike" — almost as much as she did.

As First Lady Mrs. Eisenhower entertained a steady stream of heads of state and foreign leaders, enjoying her role as White House hostess (although the White House staff felt that she directed the executive mansion with military discipline). President Eisenhower did not discuss his work with her, nor she with him; they agreed that she ran the White House while he ran the country.

In spite of a heart attack in 1955, Dwight Eisenhower ran for re-election in 1956 and won easily. Mrs. Eisenhower was worried, especially when he suffered a mild stroke in 1957, but he retired in good health in 1961. Mamie Eisenhower rejoiced to move into their farmhouse in Gettysburg, Pennsylvania — their *first* permanent home.

In 1966 the Eisenhowers celebrated their golden wedding anniversary. Two years later, President Eisenhower was hospitalized for another heart attack. Mamie Eisenhower stayed by his side until he died on March 28, 1969.

Afterward, Mrs. Eisenhower honored her husband's memory by attending celebrations in his name. On November 1, 1979, she died of a stroke at the age of eighty-three. She was buried beside Dwight Eisenhower at Abilene, Kansas.

Jackie Kennedy was known for her elegance and poise.

JACQUELINE BOUVIER KENNEDY ONASSIS
1929–1994

John F. Kennedy Administration, 1961–1963

Jacqueline Lee Bouvier, nicknamed "Jackie," was born into a wealthy, sophisticated family on July 28, 1929, in Southampton, New York. Her mother was Janet Lee Bouvier; her father, John V. Bouvier III, was a stockbroker. She grew up riding horses on the family estate in East Hampton, Long Island, and attended private schools in New York City. A creative child, she wrote and illustrated poems and stories.

When Jackie was eight, her parents separated. In 1942 her mother married Hugh D. Auchincloss, another wealthy stockbroker, and took Jackie to live on his estate near Washington, D.C. At school

Jackie was bright, but sometimes disobedient. She finished high school at Miss Porter's School in Farmington, Connecticut.

At the age of seventeen, Jackie was named the "Debutante of the Year." She went to Vassar College to study art history, then to the Sorbonne in Paris, and then to finish her degree at George Washington University. In 1952 she began working for the *Washington Times-Herald*, photo-

A five-year-old Jackie with her parents at a horse show in Southampton, Long Island

graphing and interviewing notable people in Washington. Among her subjects was Senator John F. ("Jack") Kennedy.

Both Jackie and Jack were wary of committing themselves, but she was powerfully drawn to this ambitious, charming older man. Jack was not one to fall head over heels in love, but Jackie — cultured, intelligent, and lovely — was hard to resist. Jackie and Jack were married on September 12, 1953, in Newport, Rhode Island, when she was twenty-four and he was thirty-six. The reception was a

high-society party, with 1,700 guests. After a honeymoon in Acapulco, Mexico, the Kennedys settled in Georgetown.

The Kennedys were plagued by medical problems: first there was Jack Kennedy's

The Kennedys' wedding day, September 12, 1953

almost fatal spinal operation in 1954; then Jackie Kennedy had a miscarriage in 1955; and in 1956, she gave birth to a stillborn baby. But then, happily, two children were born healthy: Caroline in 1957 and John, Jr., in November 1960.

A few weeks before John, Jr.'s, birth, John F. Kennedy had been elected president.

Moving into the White House in the spring of 1961, Mrs. Kennedy was appalled at the lack of privacy for the First Family. She tried to shelter her children, and she spent spending and refusal to attend official events that bored her, and by his relationships with other women.

In August 1963 the Kennedys were

Jack and Jackie Kennedy with a young Caroline on the beach in Hyannis Port

time with them every day, sometimes neglecting her official duties for them. She also took on the ambitious project of restoring the furnishings of the White House to reflect the periods of its history.

As First Lady, Jacqueline Kennedy set fashions in her sophisticated style of entertaining and in her elegant yet youthful style of dress. On diplomatic visits abroad, Mrs. Kennedy won goodwill with her grace and charm. But the Kennedys' marriage was strained—by her extravagant brought closer by the death of their third child, Patrick, two days after his birth. Then, that November 22, Jackie Kennedy sat beside her husband in the motorcade through Dallas as he was shot by assassin Lee Harvey Oswald. With courage and dignity, in a suit stained with President Kennedy's blood, Mrs. Kennedy stood beside Vice President Lyndon Johnson on Air Force One as he was sworn in as president. Back in Washington, she made the funeral arrangements based on Lincoln's funeral and attended the ceremonies with quiet grace, winning the admiration of the world.

Afterward, photographers and reporters hounded Mrs. Kennedy relentlessly. In 1968, her brother-in-law Robert Kennedy, campaigning for president, was also assassinated, and she feared for her children's lives. That same year, she married Aristotle Onassis, a wealthy Greek shipowner.

After Mr. Onassis's death in 1975, Jacqueline Kennedy Onassis worked in publishing in New York, as an editor. In January 1994 she discovered she had

Jackie Kennedy on Inauguration Day wearing the pillbox hat she made famous

non-Hodgkins lymphoma, a type of cancer; she died on May 19 at home. She is buried at Arlington National Cemetery, next to President Kennedy.

Mrs. Kennedy visiting JFK's grave at Arlington National Cemetery with Caroline and John, Jr., on what would have been JFK's 47th birthday

Lady Bird and Lyndon Johnson, pictured here in 1955

CLAUDIA TAYLOR JOHNSON
1912–

Lyndon B. Johnson Administration, 1963–1969

Claudia Alta Taylor, nicknamed "Lady Bird," was born to Minnie Pattillo Taylor and Thomas Jefferson Taylor in Karnack, East Texas, on December 2, 1912. When Lady Bird was five, her mother died of a bad fall, and her aunt Effie Pattillo helped raise her. Her father, a rancher and general store owner, taught his daughter about business.

Lady Bird was near the top of her class at St. Mary's Episcopal Girls' School in Austin, and also at the University of Texas in 1933.

In August 1934 she met Lyndon Baines Johnson, who was then Congressman Richard Kleberg's secretary.

Lady Bird was immediately attracted to Lyndon, and he asked her to marry him the day after their first date. She didn't accept, but she had "a queer moth-in-the-flame feeling" about him. On November 17 of that year, they were married in St. Mark's Episcopal Church in San Antonio. They rushed off to Mexico for their honeymoon and rushed back to Washington for the opening of the next session of Congress.

Lyndon Johnson was demanding; he ordered his wife around in public and even told her how to dress. But Mrs. Johnson rarely minded. She was as excited about his political career as he was, and he consulted her about his work.

Because of her sharp business sense, she handled their finances. In 1937, Lady Bird

Johnson was proud to put up the money, from her inheritance, for her husband's successful campaign for Congress. During his absence in World War II, she bought a radio station in Austin and developed it into a thriving business. The Johnsons had two daughters, Lynda Bird and Luci Baines.

In 1948 Lyndon Johnson ran for the United States Senate. Mrs. Johnson poured all her energy into his campaign, advising him about his speeches and rounding up the vote. Winning the election, he went on to become the youngest Senate Majority Leader

Lady Bird in a photo to promote the Head Start Program for underprivileged children

in United States history. To take part in her husband's career, Lady Bird Johnson took speaking lessons.

In 1960, Senator Johnson ran for vice president with John F. Kennedy. In the close campaign, Mrs. Johnson's tour of the South may have made the difference. Lady Bird Johnson continued to be a trouper as Second Lady, filling in for the president's wife at many functions. On November 22, 1963, the Johnsons were in the motorcade in Dallas when President Kennedy was shot.

As shocking as it must have been to become First Lady overnight, Lady Bird Johnson was already used to entertaining on

a big scale. When President Johnson said one morning, "Let's have Congress over this afternoon," his wife managed to be a welcoming hostess to the entire Senate and House of Representatives. As always, Lyndon Johnson talked over his work with his wife. Mrs. Johnson was especially interested in the role of women in American society, and she urged her husband to appoint women to government positions.

During President Johnson's next term, Mrs. Johnson persuaded Congress to pass the Highway Beautification Act and encouraged conservation groups. She also promoted Head Start, a federal program for disadvantaged children.

When President Johnson's achievements were overshadowed by the Vietnam War, Mrs. Johnson advised him not to run again. In 1969 the Johnsons retired to the LBJ Ranch in Texas. There they enjoyed ranch life and their grandchildren until Lyndon Johnson's death of a heart attack on January 22, 1973. After thirty-eight years of devotion to him, Lady Bird Johnson struggled with her loss.

In the following years, Mrs. Johnson served on the board of the LBJ Library in Austin, the Board of Regents of the University of Texas, and the National Parks Advisory Board. She campaigned for her son-in-law Charles S. Robb (Lynda's husband) for lieutenant governor of Virginia in 1976, and she supported the Equal Rights Amendment in 1977. In 1982 she founded the National Wildflower Research Center, and she is a trustee for the National Geographic Society and the American Conservation Association. Now in frail health, Mrs. Johnson has suffered a series of strokes.

PATRICIA RYAN NIXON
1912–1993

Richard M. Nixon Administration,
1969–1974

Pat Ryan was born Thelma Catherine Ryan on March 16, 1912, in Ely, Nevada, to Kate Halbertstadt Bender Ryan and William Ryan. Her father, a miner, called her his "St. Patrick's Day babe," and later she would make "Patricia" her legal name. Soon after her birth the family moved to Artesia, California. Pat grew up working on the family farm.

When Pat was thirteen, her mother died. Pat kept house for her father and brothers, worked on the farm, and attended Excelsior Union High School. Her father died of silicosis (miner's lung) when she was seventeen. Pat managed to work her way through the University of Southern California by cleaning offices and playing bit parts in movies. Upon graduating with honors in 1937, she taught typing at Whittier High School.

In 1938 Pat met Richard ("Dick") Nixon, a young lawyer from Whittier, through a community theater group. Pat thought Dick was "nuts or something" when he said he was going to marry her someday, but she was eventually won over by his hard work and ambition. On June 21, 1940, they were married in a Quaker service in Riverside, California.

They settled in Whittier, and Mrs. Nixon continued to teach while Mr. Nixon estab-

Pat Nixon modeling the gown she wore for the Inaugural Ball

lished his law practice. During World War II he served in the Navy, and she worked for the Office of Price Administration. Upon his return, Mr. Nixon decided to run for Congress in 1946.

Although their first child, Patricia ("Tricia"), was born in February 1946, Mrs. Nixon worked at Mr. Nixon's campaign headquarters and accompanied him as he made speeches. He won, and they moved to Washington, D.C. Their second child, Julie, was born there in 1948.

In 1952 Richard Nixon, now a senator, ran for vice president with Dwight Eisenhower. Pat Nixon hated the thought of a national campaign, even before Mr. Nixon was accused of profiting from campaign contributions. Once Mrs. Nixon was Second Lady, however, she enjoyed the travel to foreign countries. She made a good impression abroad, and even stayed cool in Latin America in 1958, as the Nixons' car was stoned by a mob.

Although Mrs. Nixon was not happy when Mr. Nixon ran for president against John Kennedy in 1960, she plunged into the exhausting campaign. She was extremely disappointed when her husband lost, but relieved to return to private life. In 1962, when Richard Nixon decided to run for governor of California, she burst into tears — but helped him campaign.

After Mr. Nixon lost that election, Pat Nixon had a reprieve from politics until

A happy Richard and Pat Nixon after his vice presidential nomination in 1952

1968, when he ran for president again. He won, and this time her tears were tears of joy.

As First Lady, Mrs. Nixon continued Jacqueline Kennedy's White House restoration project. In June 1971 the Nixons' older daughter Tricia married Edward Cox in the White House Rose Garden. (Julie, their younger daughter, had married President Eisenhower's grandson David in 1968.)

Mrs. Nixon encouraged Americans, especially women, to do volunteer work for charities and in politics. She set a good example, campaigning for her husband in the 1972 election. But soon afterward, the Watergate scandal was exposed.

In July 1974 the House Judiciary Committee recommended the adoption of the articles of impeachment. Like Eliza Johnson, Pat Nixon believed in her husband and wanted him to fight. But when he announced his resignation in August, the first president ever to resign, she departed from the White House stoically, hiding her pain and shame.

Retiring to San Clemente, California, the Nixons went into seclusion. In July 1976 Pat Nixon had a stroke that left her partly paralyzed. Her chief joy in life became her grandchildren, and in 1981 the Nixons moved to New Jersey to be near them.

The Nixons and daughter, Tricia, boarding the plane after his resignation from the presidency

On June 22, 1993, Pat Nixon died at home of lung cancer. She was buried at the Richard Nixon Library and Birthplace in Yorba Linda, California.

Betty Ford is known for being outspoken.

ᴇLIZABETH BLOOMER WARREN FORD
1918–

Gerald Ford Administration, 1974–1977

Elizabeth Anne ("Betty") Bloomer was born on April 8, 1918, in Chicago, Illinois, to William S. Bloomer, and industrial supply salesman, and Hortense Neahr Bloomer. A lively, spirited girl, Betty grew up in Grand Rapids, Michigan. She began ballet lessons at the age of eight, and dreamed of becoming a professional dancer.

In high school Betty studied dance at the Calla Travis Dance Studio. Her father died when she sixteen, and to help support the family Betty earned money by modeling and teaching dance classes. After high school she attended the Bennington School of the Dance in Vermont. In 1939 she went to New York to study with the famous dancer Martha Graham.

Finally returning to Grand Rapids, Betty taught modern dance and used dance as therapy with handicapped children. She also worked as the fashion coordinator for a department store. In 1942, at the age of twenty-four, Betty married William C. Warren, an insurance salesman in Grand Rapids. They divorced in 1947.

That August, Betty met Gerald ("Jerry") Ford, a former college football star, then a lawyer in Grand Rapids. In less than a year, they were engaged and she was working for his first campaign for Congress. Betty and

Jerry were married on October 15, 1948, at Grace Episcopal Church in Grand Rapids. After his victory at the polls, the Fords moved to Washington.

Representative Ford spent so much time at work, especially after he became Minority Leader in the House, that Betty Ford was left alone to bring up their children, Michael, John, Steven, and Susan. Suffering constant pain from a pinched nerve and arthritis, she became dependent on pain-killing drugs, and sought help for her problem from a psychiatrist.

Former President Gerald Ford and Betty Ford at the Republican National Convention in 1988

In October 1973 President Richard Nixon appointed Gerald Ford as his vice president. Betty Ford had only a few months to get used to being Second Lady, when the Watergate scandal forced President Nixon to resign in August 1974. On August 9, Betty Ford held a Bible for her husband as he took the oath of the President of the United States.

An enthusiastic backer of the women's rights movement, Mrs. Ford encouraged her husband to appoint women to his cabinet and to the Supreme Court, gave speeches in favor of the ERA (Equal Rights Amendment),

and spoke out in favor of the Supreme Court's ruling on abortion. To help other women with breast cancer, she talked in public about her own mastectomy and recovery. Some people were outraged by Mrs. Ford's frankness, but many others were delighted.

Betty Ford dancing with members of the Alvin Ailey dance company at Lincoln Center

With Mrs. Ford's encouragement, President Ford decided to run for re-election in 1976. As she toured the country for the Gerald Ford-Robert Dole ticket, supporters wore buttons proclaiming, BETTY'S HUSBAND FOR PRESIDENT.

When her husband lost the election, Betty Ford was badly disappointed. The Fords retired to Palm Springs, California, and she became depressed and, once again, dependent on painkillers, tranquilizers, and alcohol.

After rehabilitation treatment in 1978, Betty Ford spoke openly about her addiction and recovery, and she encouraged thousands of other people to get treatment. She helped found the Betty Ford Center for Drug and Alcohol Rehabilitation in Rancho Mirage, California, in 1982. In 1987, she published a book about her experience, *Betty: A Glad Awakening.* Mrs. Ford still works as chairperson of the board of the center, sometimes counseling fellow addicts.

Jimmy and Rosalynn Carter greeting a crowd

ROSALYNN SMITH CARTER

1927–

Jimmy Carter Administration, 1977–1981

Eleanor Rosalynn Smith was born in the small town of Plains, Georgia, on August 18, 1927, to Allethea ("Allie") Murray Smith and Wilburn Edgar Smith, a mechanic. Her parents were loving but strict. Rosalynn was quiet but bright, and she dreamed of seeing the world beyond Plains some day.

When Rosalyn was thirteen, her beloved father died of cancer, and the family had to struggle to pay the bills. Rosalynn, the oldest child, helped her widowed mother with her dressmaking business and with running the family.

Rosalynn graduated from high school as valedictorian, and her mother found the money to send her to Georgia Southwestern, a junior college in Americus. In June 1945, Rosalynn began dating Jimmy Carter. The Carters lived in Plains, and Rosalynn was already friends with Jimmy's sister Ruth. Still, she was awed at first by Jimmy, who was three years older, and a student at the United States Naval Academy at Annapolis.

But Jimmy was smitten with Rosalynn on their first date. They wrote every day while he was at Annapolis and she was at Georgia Southwestern. On July 7, 1946, when Rosalynn was eighteen, they were married in the Plains Methodist Church.

As Jimmy Carter served in the Navy for the next seven years, Rosalynn enjoyed her

Rosalynn Carter at a meeting of the President's Commission on Mental Health in 1977

independence from small-town life. Their moves from one navy base to another fulfilled her dream of seeing the world. The Carters' three sons were born in different places: John William ("Jack") in Virginia, James Earl ("Chip") in Hawaii, and Jeffrey in Connecticut.

In 1953 Mr. Carter left the Navy and returned to Plains to run the family peanut business. Rosalynn Carter hated to give up Navy life, but she began working with her husband to turn the failing business into a profitable one. When Jimmy Carter ran for the Georgia state senate in 1962, she managed the peanut business while he was away. The Carters' only daughter, Amy Lynn, was born in 1967.

Mrs. Carter worked enthusiastically on her husband's political campaigns — everything short of making speeches herself. When he was elected governor of Georgia in 1970, she was unnerved at first by her new responsibilities. However, she overcame her shyness and learned how to speak to large groups. She was proudest of what she accomplished in improving conditions for mentally retarded children.

When Jimmy Carter ran for president in 1976, he and Mrs. Carter each toured the country twice. Reporters dubbed Mrs. Carter a "steel magnolia" for her combination of quiet sweetness, political savvy, and drive.

In January 1977, after President Carter's inauguration ceremony, the Carters walked hand in hand down Pennsylvania Avenue to the White House. Clearly this First Couple considered themselves ordinary people — and partners. During the Carter administration, Mrs. Carter sat in on cabinet meetings and traveled to foreign countries as the president's representative. She was the first First Lady since Eleanor Roosevelt to testify before Congress on behalf of mental health programs. She also promoted the causes of the elderly and of women's rights.

During the election of 1980, President Carter stayed in Washington because of the ongoing Iranian hostage crisis. Mrs. Carter campaigned hard for him, refusing to believe he could lose until the very end when he lost to Ronald Reagan.

Back in Plains, the Carters found new ways to be partners, and new outlets for their ideals. They worked on the Carter Center at Emory University in Atlanta. They raised money for Habitat for Humanity, which builds low-cost housing. Together they wrote *Everything to Gain: Making the Most of the Rest of Your Life*, published in 1987. Mrs. Carter wrote a best-selling book of memoirs, *First Lady from Plains*, and continues to support mental health programs. In 1999 Rosalynn Smith Carter won an American Society of Journalists and Authors Outstanding Book Award for *Helping Someone with Mental Illness: A Compassionate Guide for Family, Friends, and Caregivers*.

Ronald and Nancy Reagan at the Republican National Convention after he was chosen as the candidate for the 1980 presidential election

NANCY DAVIS REAGAN
1921–

Ronald Reagan Administration, 1981–1989

Nancy Robbins was born in New York City on July 6, 1921, to Kenneth Robbins, a used-car salesman, and Edith Luckett Robbins, an actress. The baby was named Anne Frances, but always called "Nancy." Her parents separated when she was two, her mother went back to the stage, and Nancy lived with an aunt and uncle.

When Nancy was seven, in May 1929, her mother married a neurosurgeon, Dr. Loyal Davis of Chicago. To Nancy's delight, they took her to live with them. She came to regard Dr. Davis as her father.

In Chicago Nancy attended private schools and dancing classes and associated with celebrities her parents knew. The 1939 yearbook at Girls' Latin School in Chicago noted Nancy's "social perfection" — she was always well dressed and poised. She made her social debut in December 1939.

After graduating from Smith College in Massachusetts, where she had majored in drama, Nancy worked in the theater in New York. In the spring of 1949, she traveled to Hollywood for a screen test and began making movies.

That fall Nancy asked friends to introduce her to Ronald Reagan, an actor she thought was very handsome. He had just separated from his first wife, and his romance with Nancy took off gradually. But on March 4, 1952, Nancy and Ronald were married at the Little Brown Church in San Fernando Valley. The actor William Holden and his wife Ardis were best man and matron of honor.

In the next few years Nancy Reagan made several more movies, including *Hellcats of the Navy* (1957) with Ronald Reagan. But she was happy to quit acting to become a full-time wife, mother of two children (Patricia Ann

Nancy Reagan visiting students at a Florida elementary school

and Ronald Prescott), and homemaker. The Reagans socialized with wealthy business people as well as entertainment celebrities.

Nancy Reagan had never taken much interest in politics, but she was thrilled when Ronald Reagan ran for governor of California in 1966. She found her husband's campaign exciting, especially since her presence and encouragement meant so much to him. As Governor Reagan's wife, Mrs. Reagan wore designer clothes and hobnobbed with famous people. Her special project was the Foster Grandparent Program, connecting older volunteers with handicapped and mentally retarded children.

In 1980 Governor Reagan ran for president. Nancy Reagan advised him throughout the campaign. She knew her husband's optimism and talk of old-fashioned values appealed to voters, and she echoed these themes in her own speeches.

Ronald Reagan had been president barely two months when an assailant, John Hinckley, shot and almost killed him. Mrs. Reagan was terrified for her husband's life and she monitored his medical care and controlled access to him. She also managed the publicity about President Reagan's condition, emphasizing his rapid recovery.

Ronald Reagan was a popular president but Nancy Reagan was criticized at first for her expensive lifestyle. While President Reagan's administration was cutting programs for the poor, she ordered a $200,000 set of china for official entertaining. To improve her image, she made a point of promoting the Foster Grandparent Program on a national level, and she launched a campaign against drug use.

In January 1989, the Reagans retired to their ranch near Santa Barbara, California. Mrs. Reagan wrote her memoirs, *My Turn*, published in 1989, and continues to promote the "just say no" movement against drug use. In November 1994, with his wife's encouragement, Ronald Reagan announced that he had been diagnosed with Alzheimer's disease, a fatal degenerative illness. In 2001 Mrs. Reagan wrote to President George W. Bush, asking him to support embryonic stem cell research, in the hopes of finding a cure for Alzheimer's disease. She continues to care for her husband, and they celebrated their fiftieth anniversary in March 2002.

Nancy and her son, Ron, Jr., riding around the White House lawn in 1981

Former First Lady Barbara Bush is acknowledged for her literacy charity at a university in Florida

BARBARA PIERCE BUSH

1925–

George Herbert Walker Bush Administration, 1989–1993

Barbara Pierce was born in New York City on June 8, 1925, to Pauline Robinson Pierce and Marvin Pierce, president of the McCall Corporation. She spent her childhood in the suburb of Rye, New York, where she attended the Rye Country Day School. For high school Barbara was sent to Ashley Hall in Charleston, South Carolina.

During Christmas vacation of 1941, Barbara

met George Bush, a senior at Phillips Academy in Andover, Massachusetts, at a dance. George ("Poppy" in those days) and Barbara ("Bar") quickly fell in love, and their families approved. They saw each other during vacations and wrote constantly. In the summer of 1943, before Barbara entered Smith College in Massachusetts, they were engaged.

Barbara Bush at the Inaugural Ball in 1989

Thinking only about George, who was in the Navy and fighting in World War II, Barbara dropped out of Smith at the beginning of her sophomore year. During George's next leave they were married in the First Presbyterian Church in Rye on January 6, 1945, when Barbara was nineteen.

After the war George Bush finished his education at Yale, and then the Bushes moved to Texas so that he could go into the oil business. They moved from Texas to California, from town to town, and back to Texas. Meanwhile, six children were born: George W., Robin, John E. ("Jeb"), Neil, Marvin, and Dorothy. Strong, cheerful, and energetic, Mrs. Bush ran the household and family while Mr. Bush traveled.

In 1953 their daughter Robin, three years old, was diagnosed with leukemia. Mrs. Bush was devastated by Robin's death that fall. She and Mr. Bush set up a foundation for leukemia research in Robin's name.

The Bushes and the family in New Orleans for the 1988 Republican National Convention

In 1962 George Bush became involved with the Republican Party in Texas, and in 1966 he finally won a seat in Congress. As a political wife, Mrs. Bush was supportive, outgoing, and a good sport. She was also a good sport about further moves during the 1970s, caused by Mr. Bush's various appointments: United States Ambassador to the United Nations, in New York; national chairman of the Republican Party, in Washington; then, in 1974, United States envoy to China.

In 1975, Mr. Bush was recalled to the United States to become head of the Central Intelligence Agency. His job put a strain on the Bushes' close marriage, since he could not discuss his top-secret work. But Barbara Bush branched out in a positive way, touring the country with a lecture and slide presentation about China.

Barbara Bush signing copies of her memoir during a campaign stop for her son, Florida Governor Jeb Bush

In 1980 George Bush was elected vice president to Ronald Reagan. During her eight years as Second Lady, Barbara Bush made literacy, which interested her because of her son Neil's dyslexia, her special project.

When George Bush ran for president in 1988, Barbara Bush was a big asset to his campaign. With her warm, direct manner, she made voters feel she was "everybody's grandmother." She had become

a shrewd, tough-minded politician, in spite of her claim not to know "diddly" about politics. She sat in on planning sessions, and Mr. Bush talked over everything with her in private.

Barbara Bush ran a relaxed White House, full of grandchildren and dogs. She established the Barbara Bush Foundation for Family Literacy, and she urged compassion for victims of AIDS. Although Mrs. Bush never contradicted President Bush's stands in public, in private she expressed more liberal opinions on issues, including gun control.

Former First Lady Barbara Bush sitting with her daughter-in-law Laura Bush at the opening of the White House conference on school libraries

Former First Lady Barbara Bush and former President George Bush are saluted as they depart Marine One with their son and daughter-in-law

After Bill Clinton's inauguration in January 1993, the Bushes retired to Houston, Texas. Mrs. Bush's autobiography, *Barbara Bush: A Memoir*, was published in the fall of 1994, and became a bestseller.

In the same year, her son George W. was elected governor of Texas. In 2000, Barbara Bush became the only First Lady after Abigail Adams to have both a husband and a son elected president of the United States. Unlike Abigail Adams, Barbara Bush was able to be with her son in his moment of triumph.

Hillary Clinton speaking at a gathering for Kennedy Center honorees

HILLARY RODHAM CLINTON

1947–

William Jefferson Clinton Administration, 1993–2001

Hillary Diane Rodham was born on October 26, 1947, in Chicago, Illinois, to Dorothy Howell Rodham and Hugh Rodham, who ran a drapery business. She and her two younger brothers grew up in the middle-class suburb of Park Ridge, Illinois. Both parents expected their children to work hard, in school and around the house.

Athletic, smart, and confident, Hillary

was an excellent student and a leader in high school. Through activities with her Methodist youth group, she was exposed to the distressing living standards of migrant workers and people in inner-city ghettos and decided she wanted to help. She was deeply impressed by hearing Dr. Martin Luther King, Jr., speak in Chicago in 1962.

Hillary attended Wellesley College in Massachusetts, graduating with high honors in 1969. She had decided to become a lawyer, although the law profession was not welcoming to women. At Yale Law School she developed her particular interest in children and families.

In the Yale Law School Library Hillary met Bill Clinton, a law student from Arkansas. Like Hillary, Bill was bright, idealistic, and devoted to public service. He was attracted to Hillary's unusual confidence and intellect.

After Yale, Hillary worked as an attorney for the Children's Defense Fund. From the end of 1973 to August 1974, she worked for the House Judiciary Committee, evaluating the evidence for the impeachment of President Richard Nixon. After President Nixon's resignation, Hillary Rodham could have taken a high-paying job with a Wall Street law firm. Or she could have run for public office, or returned to the Children's Defense Fund.

Instead, she joined Bill Clinton to teach law at the University of Arkansas at Fayetteville. On October 11, 1975, Hillary Rodham and Bill Clinton were married in a small wedding in their new brick house near the University of Arkansas. She was twenty-seven, and he was twenty-nine.

Mr. Clinton was elected attorney general of Arkansas in 1976, and the couple moved to Little Rock, the state capital. Ms. Rodham (she had kept her last name) joined the Rose Law Firm there. She served on the board of the Legal Services Corporation, which provided legal counsel to people who could not pay for it.

In 1978 Bill Clinton was elected governor of Arkansas. Their daughter, Chelsea, was born in February 1980. That November, Governor Clinton lost his bid for re-election.

Hillary Rodham felt that her husband had lost partly because the voters of Arkansas did not want such a professional,

The Clintons attend services at First Baptist Church on Valentine's Day.

independent governor's wife. She took a leave of absence from the Rose Law Firm, announcing that she was now "Mrs. Bill Clinton." Bill Clinton won the 1982 election by a healthy margin; whether this had anything to do with her new image is impossible to say.

While Bill Clinton governed Arkansas for the next ten years, Mrs. Clinton became an influential lawyer. She worked to raise the level of education in Arkansas. She also headed the Children's Defense Fund and founded the Arkansas Advocates for Children and Families.

In 1991, the Clintons decided that Bill should run for president in 1992. During the campaign, Hillary Clinton was again attacked for being too assertive and professional, in contrast to then current First Lady Barbara Bush — the ideal wife, mother, and grandmother.

Tipper Gore and Hillary Clinton visiting a children's hospital

After Mr. Clinton won the election, he appointed Mrs. Clinton head of his Task Force on National Health Care Reform. She was exhilarated at taking on the monumental job. But many interest groups resisted any change in the health care system, and the public was confused about what the Clinton health plan would do.

By September 1994 the health care reform effort had failed, and for the next few years Hillary Clinton kept a lower profile. Nevertheless, she continued to raise public awareness of women's and children's issues and worked to ensure that all children received proper immunization. In 1996 she wrote the bestselling book *It Takes a Village*, which offered readers Hillary's ideas for creating a society that better serves and supports the nation's children.

Meanwhile, her husband's eight years in office were plagued with scandals. In 1998

Hillary Rodham Clinton testifies on Capitol Hill during a hearing on health care reform in September 1993.

President Clinton was impeached by the House of Representatives, although he was acquitted by the Senate in 1999. Meanwhile, Hillary decided to pursue her own career in politics. In 2000 she ran for the office of senator from New York and won. She was the first wife of a president to be elected to public office.

Senator Clinton greeting constituents

Senator Clinton with First Lady Laura Bush on Capitol Hill before the Senate Education Committee

New York Senator Hillary Rodham Clinton signing copies of her book, Living History

As the Clintons left the White House in 2001, Hillary moved into her quarters in the Senate Office Building. She impressed Republican as well as Democratic senators with her hard work on the committees for Environment and Public Works and for Health, Education, Labor and Pensions. She succeeded in extending unemployment insurance for the many workers hit by the economic hard times. After the attack on the World Trade Center in New York on September 11, 2001, Hillary worked to get the billions of dollars needed for cleanup and recovery. She also championed a block grant for police and fire departments around the nation.

Hillary Clinton proved herself to be such a smart, tough politician that the Democratic Party made her head of their Steering Committee. In 2003 she was appointed to the powerful Senate Armed Services Committee. In the same year, *Living History,*

Hillary's memoir of her years in the White House, became an instant bestseller.

The Clintons' daughter, Chelsea, graduated from Stanford University in 2001 and then studied at Oxford University. President and Senator Clinton live in Chappaqua, New York.

Laura Bush arriving on stage for the Presidential Inaugural Ball in 2001

LAURA WELCH BUSH

1946–

George W. Bush Administration, 2001–

Laura Lane Welch was born on November 4, 1946, to Jenna Hawkins Welch and Harold Bruce Welch, in Midland, Texas. Her father was a successful home builder, and her mother did the accounting for the business. Laura was their only child.

Laura grew up in Midland, an oil boom town on the hot, dusty plains of West Texas.

Her mother read to her from the time she was a baby, and reading became one of Laura's favorite activities. By the age of seven Laura knew she wanted to be a teacher, just like the one she had in second grade. Playing at home, Laura would line her dolls up on her bedroom floor and pretend to teach them.

A bright, sweet-natured girl, Laura was popular with her peers as well as her teachers. She earned high marks in school, and she enjoyed swimming and hiking as well as reading. In 1964 Laura graduated from high school and left Midland for Southern Methodist University in Dallas, Texas, where she majored in elementary education.

Graduating in 1968, Laura taught in elementary schools for a few years before going back to school. She attended the University of Texas, Austin, and earned a master's degree in library science. By the summer of 1977, Laura was happy in her work as a school librarian in Austin.

On Laura's frequent trips back to Midland, her childhood friend Jan O'Neill repeatedly tried to introduce her to George W. Bush. Although George had spent much of his childhood in Midland, the two had never met. At first, getting to know George Bush was unappealing to Laura. She had no interest in politics, and the Bushes were very political. At the time, George himself was running for Congress. Finally, though, Laura attended a barbecue at the O'Neills where she met the "Bombastic Bushkin," as George's friends called him.

The two were immediately taken with each other. George thought Laura was beautiful, smart, and a great listener. Laura loved the way George made her laugh.

Three months later, Laura and George were married at the First Methodist Church of Midland.

Immediately Laura joined George's campaign for U.S. representative. George promised quiet, reserved Laura that she'd never have to give a speech by herself. But not long after, Laura found herself alone on the courthouse steps of a town named Muleshoe, stumbling through her first political speech.

George lost that election, and for some years he pulled back from a political career. Instead, he concentrated first on his oil drilling company and then on managing the

Laura Bush answering questions from third graders after reading to them in a Cincinnati elementary school in 2003

Texas Rangers. However, George did help his father, George H. W. Bush, campaign for vice president in 1980 and 1984, and for president in 1988 and 1992.

During this time, Laura and George decided they very much wanted to have children. In 1981, they were delighted when Laura gave birth to twin girls. She and George named them Barbara and Jenna, after the girls' grandmothers.

In 1994, George W. Bush plunged back into politics to run for governor of Texas. When he was elected, Laura didn't expect to be an active First Lady of the state. But she quickly realized she could use the position to push her favorite causes, literacy and education. She helped found and run the very successful Texas Book Festival, and she promoted early childhood literacy programs.

Almost as soon as Laura had gotten used to being First Lady of Texas, George W. Bush decided to run for president in 2000. Laura was hesitant to sacrifice their privacy for a national campaign, but she believed in George's mission and promised to help any way she could. By now she was a capable,

appealing speaker, and she helped draw women and moderate voters to George's party. Her speech opening the Republican National Convention in August 2000 was a big hit.

Laura Bush handing out books to children before the launch of the first National Book Festival in 2001

Though the Democrats and the Republicans contested the results of the election for weeks, Laura Welch Bush became First Lady of the United States in January 2001. As in Texas, she used her high-profile position to promote literacy and education. She launched a national initiative called Ready to Read, Ready to Learn; she hosted the first White House conference on school libraries; and she proposed a $10 million program to recruit more librarians. Laura

Laura Bush shows off the White House gingerbread house.

hosted a National Book Festival in 2001 and repeated that success in 2002 and 2003. She also used her influence to encourage more U.S. spending on education around the world.

Unfortunately, the first years of President Bush's administration were troubled. On September 11, 2001, the country was stunned by terrorist attacks on New York and Washington, D.C. The United States responded early in 2002 by sending troops to Afghanistan, where members of Al Qaeda — the group believed responsible for the attacks — were hiding. Laura explained on *Larry King Live* that she felt she had "the opportunity, or maybe I should say the

Laura Bush and former Senator Bob Dole watch as President Bush places a wreath on the Tomb of the Unknowns at Arlington National Cemetery on Memorial Day 2003.

Laura Bush using President Bush's weekly radio address to speak out against the oppression of women under the Taliban regime in Afghanistan

responsibility, to be steady for our country — and for my husband." She took on a more public role, appearing at memorial services, vigils, and the World Trade Center itself, and speaking out on issues such as the plight of women in Afghanistan.

Later in the spring of 2003, the United States invaded Iraq to remove dictator Saddam Hussein. By the fall of 2003, U.S. soldiers were still in Iraq, and Americans were fearful of more terrorist attacks. The economy was slow, while the cost of military actions and Homeland Security drained money from programs at home. Even state and city funding for schools and libraries, Laura's biggest initiatives, were reduced.

Although President Bush's standing in the polls dropped off, First Lady Laura Bush continued to be very popular. In interviews and public appearances she remained a comforting presence for the nation, as she always had been for her husband. Now Laura could support George W. Bush once more by campaigning for his re-election in 2004.

ABOUT THE AUTHOR

Beatrice Gormley is the author of many novels and biographies for young people. Her books about First Ladies include *Laura Bush: America's First Lady* and *Jacqueline Kennedy Onassis: Friend of the Arts*. She has written many novels for Scholastic, including *Back to the Titanic!*, *Back to Paul Revere!*, and *Back to the Day Lincoln Was Shot!*

Beatrice Gormley lives in Westport, Massachusetts, with her husband, Robert Gormley.

The White House is a symbol of patriotism and cooperation between nations, but it is also a place that First Ladies for generations have called home.

Read more Scholastic books about the White House:

White House

The Story of the White House
Kate Waters

Mr. President: A Book of U.S. Presidents
George Sullivan

The Scholastic Encyclopedia of the Presidents and Their Times
David Rubel

The White House: An Illustrated History
Catherine O'Neill Grace